The Present State of Music in France and Italy

PRESENT STATE

OF

MUSIC

IN

FRANCE and ITALY:

OR,

The JOURNAL of a TOUR through thofe
Countries, undertaken to collect Materials for
A GENERAL HISTORY OF MUSIC.

By CHARLES BURNEY, Muf. D.

Eı cantarono allor ſi dolcemente,
Che la dolcezza ancor dentro mi ſuona

DANTE, Purg Canto 2do.

LONDON,

Printed for T. BECKET and Co. in the Strand.
MDCCLXXI

[It is difficult to write about the arts without using terms
of art, but though few foreign words, or technical terms,
will occur in this Journal, which are not tranflated or defined the firft time they are ufed, yet, to fave the reader
the trouble of feeking them in the text, or of remember-
ing them, the following are collected and explained here]

EXPLICATION

OF

Some MUSICAL TERMS and FOREIGN WORDS,

which occur in the following JOURNAL.

ACCADEMIA, a concert.
 Adagio, flow, in the firft degree ; or, when ufed
  fubftantively, it fignifies a flow movement.
Allegro, gay, or a quick movement.
Appoggiatura, from *appoggiare*, to lean on ; a note of
  embelhfhment, it is ufually written in a
  fmall character, as not effential to the harmony, though moft effential to melody, tafte,
  and expreffion.

Baritono, a voice of low pitch, between a tenor and
  bafe.
Bravura, as *aria di bravura*, a quick fong of difficult execution.

Canon, a compofition in which the parts follow
  - each other in the fame melody and intervals.
Canto fermo, plain fong, or chanting in the cathedral fervice.

          Canzone,

Canzone, a fong.

Centr' Alto, counter-tenor, or a voice of higher pitch than the tenor, but lower than the treble.

Contrapuntifta, one fkilled in the laws of harmony, a compofer.

Contrapunto, counterpoint; compofition in parts: this term came from the firft mufic in parts, being expreffed in points placed over each other

Dilettante, a gentleman compofer or performer, fynonimous with the French word *amateur*.

Diminuendo, diminifhing a found, or rendering it fofter and fofter by degrees.

Due Cori, two choirs, orcheftras, or choruffes.

Expreffion, the performing a piece of melody, or a fingle paffage, with that energy and feeling which the poetry or paffion, to be impreffed upon the hearer, requires.

Forte, loud.

Fugue, a flight and purfuit, a *fugue* differs from a *canon* only in being lefs rigid in its laws, a *canon* is a perpetual *fugue* the firft, or leading part gives the law to the reft in both, but, in the courfe of a *fugue*, it is allowable to introduce epifodes and new fubjects

Funzione, function, ceremony in the church on a feftival

Graduale,

Graduale, gradual; an appellation given, in the Romish church, to a verse which is sung after the epistle, and which was anciently sung on the steps of the altar.

Harmony, music in parts, in opposition to melody.

Imitation, a slight species of *fugue*, in which the parts imitate each other, though not in the same intervals, or according to the rigorous laws of a *fugue* or *canon*.

Improvvisatrice, a female who pronounces verses extempore.

Intermezzo, an interlude, or musical farce, usually performed between the acts of a serious piece.

Laudisti, psalm singers.

Maestro di Capella, a composer, or one who directs a musical performance in a church or chapel.

Maestro del Coro, master of the choir.

Melody, an air, or single part, without base or accompaniment.

Massa Bassa, a silent mass, whispered by the priest during a musical performance.

Mezzo Soprano, a second treble, or voice between the treble and counter-tenor.

Miserere, the first word of the 51st Psalm, in Latin.

Modulation, the art of changing the key, or of conducting the harmony or melody into different keys, in a manner agreeable to the ear, and conformable to established rules.

Motetto,

Motetto, Motet, a Latin hymn, pfalm, or anthem.

Mufico, a general term for mufician; but now chiefly applied in Italy to a *caftrato.*

Offertorio, Offertory, an anthem fung, or a voluntary played, at the time the people are making an offering.

Piano, foft.

Plain chant, plain fong, or chanting.

Portamento, conduct of the voice : the *portamento* is faid to be good, when the voice is neither nafal nor guttural.

Ritornello, originally the echo or repetition of any portion of a fong by the inftruments; but, in procefs of time, it became the general term for fymphony, in which fenfe it will be often ufed in this Journal, and which will, perhaps, be called, *Verbum movere loco* ; but though the word *Ritornel* is rather obfolete, and has for fome time been fupplied by fymphony, it now wants revival, as fymphony, among modern muficians, is ufually fynonymous with overture.

Saltatori, jumpers, or dancers of uncommon agility.

Siftine, the Pope's chapel is fometimes called the *Siftine* chapel, from Sextus Quintus, who built it.

Soprano, the fupreme, or treble, part in vocal compofitions.

Softenuto,

Softenuto, fuftained; or, ufed fubftantively, the power of continuing a found: in this cafe the harpfichord has no *Softenuto,* the organ has one.

Steiner, the name of a famous German maker of violins.

Sinfonia, fymphony, or overture.

Tafte, the adding, diminifhing, or changing a melody, or paffage, with judgment and propriety, and in fuch a manner as to *improve* it if this were rendered an invariable rule in what is commonly called *gracing,* the paffages, in compofitions of the firft clafs, would feldom be changed.

Virtù, talents, abilities, hence

Virtuofo, a performer

Voce di Camera, a feeble voice, fit only for a chamber.

Voce di Petto, a voice which comes from the breaft, in oppofition to one that is nafal or guttural.

Vox Humana, human voice.

THE

INTRODUCTION.

AMONG the numerous accounts of Italy, published by travellers who have visited that delightful country, from different motives of interest or curiosity; it is somewhat exraordinary, that none have hitherto confined their views and researches to the rise and progress, or present state of music in that part of the world, where it has been cultivated with such success; and from whence the rest of Europe has been furnished, not only with the most eminent composers and performers, but even with all its ideas of whatever is elegant and refined in that art.

Not

Not a single picture, statue, or building has been left undescribed, or an inscription uncopied, and yet neither the *Conservatorios* or musical schools, the *operas*, or the *oratorios*, have scarce been mentioned: and though every library is crowded with histories of painting and other arts, as well as with the lives of their most illustrious professors; music and musicians have been utterly neglected. And this is still the more unaccountable, as no one of the liberal arts is at present so much cultivated, nor can the Italians now boast a superiority over the rest of Europe in any thing, so much as in their musical productions and performances; for neither their painters, sculptors, or architects, historians, poets, or philosophers of the present age, as in some centuries past, so greatly surpass their cotemporaries on this side the Alps, as to excite much curiosity to visit or converse with them.

But music still *lives* in Italy, while the other arts only speak a *dead language;*
classical

claffical and learned indeed, but lefs pleafing and profitable to ftudents than in the days of Leo X when Italy was perhaps as fuperior to the reft of the world, and therefore as well worth vifiting, as Greece was in the time of Pericles or Alexander.

To fay that mufic was never in fuch high eftimation, or fo well underftood as it is at prefent, all over Europe, would be only advancing a fact as evident, as that its inhabitants are now more generally civilized and refined, than in any other period of the hiftory of mankind.

Perhaps the grave and wife may regard mufic as a frivolous and enervating luxury; but, in its defence, Montefquieu has faid that " it is the only one of all the arts which does not corrupt the mind" *. Electricity is univerfally allowed to be a very entertaining and furprifing phenomenon, but it has frequently been la-

* Efprit des Loix.

mented

mented that it has never yet, with much certainty, been applied to any very useful purpose. The same reflexion has often been made, no doubt, as to music. It is a charming resource, in an idle hour, to the rich and luxurious part of the world. But say the sour and the worldly, what is its use to the rest of mankind? To this it may be answered, that, in England, perhaps more than in any other country, it is easy to point out the humane and important purposes to which it has been applied. Its assistance has been called in by the most respectable profession in this kingdom, in order to open the purses of the affluent for the support of the distressed offspring of their deceased brethren *. Many an orphan is cherished by its influence †.—The pangs of child-birth are softened and rendered less dangerous

* At the *Feast of the Sons of the Clergy.*
† The Messiah is annually performed for the benefit of the *Foundling Hospital.*

and

and dreadful by the effects of its power *. It helps, perhaps, to ftop the ravages of a difeafe which attacks the very fource of life †. And, laftly, it enables its own profeffors to do what few others can boaft — to maintain their own poor : by that admirable and well-directed inftitution, known by the name of *The Society for the Support of decayed Muficians and their Families.*

Mufic has indeed ever been the delight of accomplifhed princes, and the moft elegant amufement of polite courts : but at prefent it is fo combined with things facred and important, as well as with our pleafures, that mankind feems wholly unable to fubfift without it : it forms a confiderable part of divine fervice in our churches : it is effential to military dif-cipline ; and the theatres would languifh

* The benefit every year for the *Lying-in Hof-pital*, Brownlow ftreet.

† The mufical performance for the *Lock Hof-pital.*

without

without it. Add to this, that there is hardly a private family in a civilized nation without its flute, its fiddle, its harpsichord, or guitar: that it alleviates labour and mitigates pain; and is still a greater blessing to humanity, when it keeps us out of mischief, or blunts the edge of care.

Had the books I have hitherto consulted, which have been very numerous, supplied me with the information I wanted relative to a history of music, upon which I have been long meditating, I should not have undertaken a journey that has been attended with much fatigue, expence, and neglect of other concerns.

But these books are, in general, such faithful copies of each other, that he who reads two or three, has the substance of as many hundred. In hopes, therefore, of stamping on my intended history some marks of originality, or at least of novelty, I determined to allay my thirst of knowledge at the source,

and

and take such draughts in Italy, as England cannot supply. It was there I determined to hear with my *own* ears, and to see with my *own* eyes; and, if poffible, to *hear* and *fee* nothing but *mufic*. Indeed I could have amufed myfelf agreeably enough in examining pictures, ftatues, and buildings, but as I could not afford time for all this, without neglecting the chief bufinefs of my journey, I determined not to have " my purpofe turned awry" by any other curiofity or enquiry *.

With thefe views I left London in the beginning of June 1770, and as I did not intend my work fhould be local, I determined in the way to Italy to acquire what materials I could relative to the hiftory of French mufic, as well as to inform

---

* In the courfe of my journey, however, I was afterwards much pleafed to find that I could gratify my love for fculpture and painting even in the purfuit of mufical materials, as it was from thefe I acquired my ideas and drawings of the inftruments of the ancients as well as of the early moderns.

my-

myſelf of its preſent ſtate. But it would have been both arrogant and unjuſt to have attempted this in the few weeks allowed me to remain in France, had I not before twice viſited Paris, during which time I frequented very much its public places ; and for twenty years paſt I had conſtantly been ſupplied with the works of the beſt compoſers, and the writings of the beſt authors on the ſubject of muſic in that kingdom.

THE

THE
PRESENT STATE
OF
MUSIC, &c.

LISLE.

AS I made no confiderable ftop till I
reached this city, the capital of
French Flanders, I here began my
enquiries, and firft tried to difcover the
manner of performing the Gregorian
chant, which fubfifts throughout France
in all cathedrals and collegiate churches.
It is oftener perfoimed without the organ
than with ; and though they have organs
in every large church in this town, and
throughout the kingdom, I find they are

only

only ufed as in our parifh churches, on
Sundays, and on great feftivals. It appears plainly to me that our old chants
and refponfes were not new compofitions
by Tallis, at the time of the reformation,
but only adjufted to Englifh words; the
little melody they contain being very
nearly the fame as in all catholic churches
abroad. It is only on Sundays and feftivals that parts are added to the *canto fermo*
or *plain chant* here. All fing at other
times in unifon. All the books out of
which the priefts chant, are written upon
vellum in the Gregorian note, that is, in
the old black lozenge, or fquare character,
upon four lines and fpaces only. But in
order to inform myfelf ftill further on the
fubject, I found it neceffary to make myfelf acquainted with M. Devillers, an
agreeable and intelligent man in his profeffion, and organift of the principal
church here, that of St. Peter. With
him I had a long converfation relative to
the ufe of *plain chant*. He fays the boys
are

are taught it by the Gregorian notes, and
that no others are used by the ecclefiaftics.

In the French churches there is an inftrument on each fide the choir, called
the *ferpent*, from its fhape, I fuppofe,
for it undulates like one. This gives
the *tone* in chanting, and plays the bafe
when they fing in parts. It is often ill-
played, but if judicioufly ufed, would
have a good effect. It is, however, in
general overblown, and too powerful for
the voices it accompanies; otherwife, it
mixes with them better than the organ;
as it can augment or diminifh a found
with more delicacy, and is lefs likely to
overpower or deftroy by a bad temperament, that perfect one, of which the
voice only is capable.

The organ in this church is double, and
very large, confifting of four rows of keys,
fixty four ftops, and an immenfe front of
thirteen columns of pipes: it has been
made about fixty years. The cafe is
finely carved and ornamented, and the
front

front pipes of the white and natural co-
lour of the metal, as they are in all the
organs here. In England it is neceffary
to gild them, to prevent their turning
black. I have always found that but
little ufe is made of the organ in France,
even on thofe days when it is moft employed. The *ferpent* keeps the voices up
their pitch, and is a kind of crutch for
them to lean on.

As it was Jubilee-Time * when I was
at Lifle, I had hopes of hearing better
mufic than ordinary, but was difappointed.

M. Anneufe, organift of the church of St.
Maurice in this town, is blind. I called at
his houfe ; but he was from home, other-

* The name of jubilee is ufually given to an
ecclefiaftical folemnity, or ceremony performed, in
order to gain a plenary indulgence from the pope.
There are, however, particular jubilees in fome
cities, upon the concurrence of certain feftivals, as
when the feaft of the Annunciation happens on
Good Friday , or that of St John the Baptift, on
Corpus Chrifti day. Encyclop. Art. Jubilee.

wife

wife I would have had some conversation
with him on the subject of his profession.
For I found the shortest and best road to
such information as I wanted, was to talk
with the principal professors, wherever I
went. Learned men and books may be more
useful as to ancient music, but it is only
living musicians that can explain what
living music is. This method, however,
where I had no letters of recommendation, cost me a little money, some assu-
rance, and a great deal of trouble.

Those who visit Italy for the sake of
painting, sculpture, or architecture, do
well to see what those arts afford in
France, first; as they become so dainty
afterwards, that they can bear to look at
but few things that kingdom affords; and
as I expected to have the same preju-
dices, or feelings at my return, about
their music, I endeavoured to give it a
fair hearing first, in the capital, and the
two extremities of the kingdom, Paris,
Lisle, and Lyons. I stopped at Cambray,
                                    visited

vifited the churches there, in hopes of
hearing mufic, but was difappointed;
the fervice was performed entirely without chant or organ. I was told there
would be finging in the afternoon, but
was unable to ftay. Indeed the character
given of the voices by fome of the
inhabitants did not tempt me, fo I went
on directly to

P A.R I S.

And here, after fpending the greateft
part of the firft day in fearch of books,
I went in the evening, June 12, to the
Boulevard, as no better entertainment
offered itfelf either at the play-houfe or
opera. The Boulevard is a place of public diverfions, without the gates of Paris.
It is laid out in walks, and planted. In
the middle is a wide road for carriages,
and at the fides are coffee-houfes, conju-
rors, and fhows of all kinds. Here every
evening, during fummer, the walks are
crowded with well-dreffed people and the

road

road with fplendid equipages; and here
I faw the new Vauxhall, as they call it,
but it is no more like ours, than the emperor of China's palace. Nor is it at all like
Ranelagh; though, at the firft entrance,
there is a fmall rotund, with galleries
round it well lighted up, and decorated.
Next to this is a quadrangle in the open
air, where they dance in warm weather;
it is illuminated, and has galleries, which
are continued to another room, which is
fquare, and ftill larger than the firft,
with two rows of corinthian pillars ornamented with feftoons and illuminations.
This is a very elegant room, in which are
minuets, allemandes, cotillons, and *contre
danfes,* when the weather is cold, which
was now the cafe in the extreme. However,
here was a great crowd of well-dreffed
people. From the name of this place it
was natural to look for a garden, but
none was to be found.

In the coffee-houfes on the Boulevard,
which are much frequented, there are bands

of

of mufic, and finging, in the Sadler's-Wells way, but worfe. The women who perform there, go about with a plate to collect a reward for their trouble. Here, though they often fing airs *a l' Italienne*, original fin, in the expreffion, fticks as clofe to them as to us, at fuch places, in England.

Wednefday 13. This morning I fpent in the library of the *College Des Quatre nations*, founded by cardinal Mazarin. It is a noble one. I confulted the catalogues, and found feveral of the books I wanted.

In the evening I heard two pieces performed at the *Theatre Italien*, in which the finging was the worft part. Though the modern French compofers hazard every thing that has been attempted by the Italians, yet it is ill executed, and fo ill underftood by the audience, that it makes no impreffion. *Bravura* fongs, or fongs of execution, are now attempted ; but

but they are so ill performed, that no one used to true Italian singing can like any thing but the words and action. One of these pieces was new, and meant as a comic opera, in all its modern French forms of Italian music, (that is, music composed in the Italian style) to French words. No recitative, all the dialogue and narrative part being spoken. And this piece was as thoroughly d---d as ever piece was here. I used to imagine that a French audience durst not hiss to the degree I found they did upon this occasion. Indeed quite as much, mixt with horse laughs, as ever I heard at Drury Lane, or Covent Garden. In short, it was condemned in all the English forms, except breaking the benches and the actors heads; and the incessant sound of *hish* instead of *hiss*. The author of the words, luckily, or rather judiciously, lay concealed, but the composer, M. de St. Amant, was very much to be pitied, for a great deal

C of

of real good mufic was thrown away upon
bad words, and upon an audience not
at all difpofed, efpecially in the two
laft acts (there were three) to hear any
thing fairly. But this mufic, though
I thought it much fuperiour to the
poetry it accompanied, was not without
its defects; the modulation was too
ftudied, fo much fo as to be unnatural, and always to difappoint the ear.
The overture however was good mufic,
full of found harmony, elegant and
pleafing melody, with many paffages of
effect. The hautbois at this theatre is
admirable; I hardly ever heard a more
pleafing tone or manner of playing. Several of the fongs would have been admirable too, if they had been fung with
the true Italian expreffion. But the
French voice never comes further than
from the throat; there is no *voce di
petto*, no true *portamento* or direction of
the voice, on any of the ftages. And
though feveral of the fingers in this
theatre

theatre are Italians, they are fo degenerated fince they came hither, that if I
had not been affured of it, their performance would have convinced me
of the contrary. The new piece had
feveral movements in it very like what
is heard at the ferious opera. (It
muft be remembered that the whole
was in verfe, and extremely ferious,
except fome attempt at humour in * Calliot's part) which, however, did not
prevent the audience from pronouncing
it to be *deteftable*.

Thurfday 14. This being *Fête Dieu*,
or *Corpus Chrifti* Day, one of the greateft
holidays in the whole year, I went to
fee the proceffions, and to hear high mafs
performed at Notre Dame. I had great
difficulty to get thither. Coaches are not

---

* M Calliot is defervedly the favourite actor and
finger of the comic opera at Paris His voice,
which he can make a bafe or a tenor at pleafure,
is admirable, and he is in all refpects a moft interefting and entertaining performer,

allowed

allowed to ftir till all the proceffions,
with which the whole town fwarms, are
over. The ftreets through which they
are to pafs in the way to the churches,
are all lined with tapeftry; or, for want
of that, with bed curtains and old petticoats. I find the better fort of people,
(les gens comme il faut) all go out of
town on thefe days, to avoid the *embarras*
of going to mafs, or the *ennui* of ftaying
at home. Whenever the hoft ftops,
which frequently happens, the priefts
fing a pfalm, and all the people fall on
their knees in the middle of the ftreet,
whether dirty or clean. I readily com-
plied with this ceremony rather than give
offence or become remarkable. Indeed,
when I went out, I determined to do as
other people did, in the ftreets and
church, otherwife I had no bufinefs
there; fo that I found it incumbent on
me to kneel down twenty times ere I
reached Notre Dame. This I was the lefs
hurt at, as I faw it quite general;
and

and many much better dreffed people than myfelf, almoft proftrated themfelves, while I only touched the ground with one knee. At length I reached the church, where I was likewife a *conformift*; though here I walked about frequently, as I faw others do, round the choir and in the great aifle. I made my remarks on the organ, organift, plain-chant, and motets. Though this was fo great a feftival, the organ accompanied the choir but little. The chief ufe made of it, was to play over the chant before it was fung, all through the Pfalms. Upon enquiring of a young abbé, whom I took with me as a *nomenclator*, what this was called ? *C'eft profer*, 'Tis profing, he faid. And it fhould feem as if our word *profing* came from this dull and heavy manner of recital. The organ is a good one, but when played full, the echo and reverberation were fo ftrong, that it was all confufion ; however, on the choir organ and echo ftops I could hear every paf-

fage

ſage diſtinctly. The organiſt has a neat and judicious way of touching the inſtrument; but his paſſages were very old faſhioned. Indeed what he played during the *offertorio*, which laſted ſix or eight minutes, ſeemed too ſtiff and regular for a voluntary. Several *motets*, or ſervices, were performed by the choir, but accompanied oftener by the *ſerpent* than organ: though, at my firſt entrance into the French churches, I have frequently taken the *ſerpent* for an organ, but ſoon found it had in its effect ſomething better and ſomething worſe than that inſtrument. Theſe compoſitions are much in the way of our old church ſervices, full of fugues and imitation; more contrivance and labour than melody. I am more and more convinced every day, that what I before obſerved concerning the adapting the Engliſh words to the old *canto fermo*, by Tallis, at the Reformation, is true; and it ſeems to me that muſic, in our cathedral

dral

dral fervice, was lefs reformed than any other part of the liturgy.

At five o'clock I went to the *Concert Spirituel*, the only public amufement allowed on thefe great feftivals. It is a grand concert performed in the great hall of the Louvre, in which the vocal confifts of detached pieces of church mufic in Latin *. I fhall name the feveral performances of this concert, and fairly fay what effect each had upon myfelf, and upon the audience, as far as a ftander-by could difcover. The firft piece was a motet by M. De la Lande, *Dominus regnavit*, chiefly made up of choruffes, performed with more force than feeling ; the whole was in the ftyle of the old French

* The French have never yet had either a ferious Italian opera or a regular oratorio of any fort performed in their country. I fuppofe the managers of their public diverfions know too well the tafte of the people to attempt them, though every other fpecies of novelty is tried, and they even fuffer Italian to be *fpoken* by feveral of the characters in the Harlequin pieces

opera;

opera ; and, except the fecond chorus, which had a conduct and fpirit fomewhat new and agreeable, to me deteftable, though much applauded by the audience, who felt and admired it as much as them-felves, for being natives of a country able to produce fuch mafter-pieces of compo-fition, and fuch exquifite performers. Then a concerto on the hautbois by Bez-zozi, nephew to the celebrated hautbois and baffoon players of that name at Turin. For the honour of the French, I muft needs fay that this piece was very much ap-plauded. It is a ftep towards reforma-tion, to begin to tolerate what ought to be adopted. This performer has many points in his tafte and expreffion that are truly exquifite ; but I think he is not conftantly perfect. He makes great ufe of his tongue in divifions, which perhaps occafions a more frequent crack or cackle in the reed than one would wifh, neither is his tone very powerful without forc-

ing,

ing, which, as this was a large room, he perhaps thought neceffary. Upon the whole, however, I was very much delighted with his performance. But it is not eafy to account for the latitude the French take in their approbation, or to fuppofe it poffible for people to like things as oppofite as light and darknefs. If French mufic is good, and its expreffion natural and pleafing, that of Italy muft be bad : or change the fuppofition, and allow that of Italy to be all which an unprejudiced, but cultivated ear could wifh; the French mufic cannot, one would imagine, give fuch an ear equal delight. The truth is, the French do not like Italian mufic, they pretend to adopt and admire it; but it is all mere affectation. After this high-finifhed performance of Bezozzi Mademoifelle Delcambre fcreamed out *Exaudi Deus* with all the power of lungs fhe could mufter; and was as well received as if Bezzozi had
done

done nothing. After this Signor Tra-
verſa, firſt violin to the prince de Carig-
nan, played a concerto in the Italian
ſtyle very well; many parts with great
delicacy, good tone, and facility of execution: but this was not ſo well reliſhed as
the *Exaudi* that went before it. Nay, I
could plainly diſcover, by their countenances and reception of it, how little
they had felt it. Madame Philidor ſung
a *motet* next, of her huſband's compoſition, who drinks hard at the Italian
fountain; but though this was more like
good ſinging and good muſic than any
vocal piece that had preceded it, yet it
was not applauded with that fury, which
leaves not the leaſt doubt of its having
been felt. The whole was finiſhed by
Beatus Vir, a motet, in grand chorus, with
ſolo and duet parts between. The principal counter-tenor had a ſolo verſe in it
which he bellowed out with as much
violence as if he had done it for life,

7

while

while a knife was at his throat. But though this wholly ftunned me, I plainly *faw*, by the fmiles of ineffable fatisfaction which were vifible in the countenances of ninety-nine out of a hundred of the company, and *heard*, by the moft violent applaufe that a ravifhed audience could beftow, that it was quite what their hearts felt, and their fouls loved. '*C'eft fuperbe!* was echoed from one to the other through the whole houfe. But the laft chorus was a *finifher* with a vengeance! it furpaffed, in clamour, all the noifes I had ever heard in my life. I have frequently thought the choruffes of our oratorios rather too loud and violent; but, compared with thefe, they are *foft mufic*, fuch as might footh and lull to fleep the héroine of a tragedy.

Friday 15   In vifiting the king of France's library this morning, I found that if I could have contented myfelf with

with the *dead letter* of information, fuch as is to be obtained from books only, I need not to have croffed the Alps; as the number to be found here, relative to my fubject, is almoft infinite. The MSS. were what I firft enquired after of the librarian, and I found that the mere catalogue of thefe alone amounted to four volumes in folio; not all about mufic indeed, but that fcience has not been neglected by the collectors of thefe books. The moft ancient MSS. in which mufic has any concern, if we except the feven Greek authors publifhed by Meibomius, which are all here in MS. are the liturgies and offices of the church, fuch as miffals, rituals, graduals, breviaries, and pfalters, in Greek and Latin; but of thefe when I come to treat of the mufic of paft times. Of its prefent ftate *here,* I thought I could get no better information than was to be acquired by going to the opera of Zaide, which was performed this evening at the new opera-houfe ad-

joining

joining to, or rather being part of the *Palais Royal* belonging to the duke of Orleans. The former theatre was burnt down about six years ago, during which time the opera was performed in the king's palace of the Louvre, where the *Concert Spirituel* is still held *. The opera of to-night was first performed in 1739; revived again in 1745, 1756, and now, for the fourth time, in 1770. It is called by the French *ballet-heroïque*, or heroic dance, the dances being interwoven, and making an essential part of the piece. I believe in all such pieces, the interest of the drama is very inconsiderable; at least, if we may judge by this, and some of those composed by Rameau.

* One of the finest sights at Paris used then to be the Tuilleries in summer, after the opera, which being over between seven and eight in the evening, all the company, in full dress, consisting of the flower of this capital, poured into the grand avenue *totis vomit Ædibus undam*, and formed an assembly not to be met with in any other part of the world.

The

The mufic of Zaide is by Royer; and it is fomewhat wonderful that nothing better, or of a more modern tafte, has been compofed fince, the ftyle of compofition is totally changed throughout the reft of Europe; yet the French, commonly accufed of more levity and caprice than their neighbours, have ftood ftill in mufic for thirty or forty years : nay, one may go ftill further, and affert boldly, that it has undergone few changes at the great opera fince Lulli's time, that is to fay, in one hundred years. In fhort, notwithftanding they can both talk and write fo well, and fo much *about it*, mufic in France, with refpect to the two great effentials of melody and expreffion *, may ftill be faid to be in its infancy.

But to return to M. Royer's *opera* of Zaide, which, in point of melody, of light and fhade, or contraft, and of effect,

* The Italian mufic, fays M D'Alembert, is a language of which we have not yet the alphabet.

Melange de Litter.

is

is miferable, and below all criticifm : but, at the fame time it muft be allowed that the theatre is elegant and noble; that the dreffes and decorations are fine; the machinery ingenious; and the danceing excellent: but, alas! thefe are all objects for the eye, and an opera elfewhere is intended to flatter the ear. A mufical drama, which has nothing interrefting in the words, and of which the mufic is bad, and the finging worfe, muft furely fall fhort of every idea that has been formed in other countries of fuch a fpecies of exhibition.

Three out of five of the principal fingers in Zaide, I had heard at the *Concert Spirituel.* Meffieurs Gelin and Le Gros, and Mademoifelle du Bois; the other two were M and Mad. L'Arrivée; in their manner of finging much like the reft. One thing I find here, which makes me grieve at the abufe of nature's bounty, the voices are in themfelves really good and well toned; and this is eafily to be difcovered,

covered, in defpight of falfe direction and a vitiated expreffion. But of this enough has already been faid: a word or two more about their compofition, and I have done with their mufic for fome time; at leaft with their expreffion: for they have fome compofers of great merit among them, who imitate very fuccefs-fully the Italian ftyle. But it is in vain, at leaft for the natives of France; other nations may indeed be the better for it, but let this deteftable and unnatural ex-preffion be given to any mufic in the world, and it becomes immediately French. One may apply to French fing-ers, what Dryden faid of Mac Flecno's wit—

Sound pafs'd thro' them no longer is the fame;
As food digefted takes a different name.

But it feems to be with the ferious French opera here, as it is with our oratorios in England; people are tired of the old by hearing them fo often; the ftyle has been pufhed perhaps to its utmoft boun-

dary,

dary, and is exhausted; and yet they cannot relish any new attempts at pleasing them in a different way: what is there in this world not subject to change? And shall we expect music to be permanent above *all* things, which so much depends on imagination and feeling?

There are particular periods, that one would perhaps wish to stop at, if it were possible; but as that cannot be, let us comply with necessity, in good humour, and with a good grace. Poetry, painting, and sculpture have had their rise and declension: have sunk into barbarism: have emerged from it in succeeding ages, and mounted to a certain degree of perfection, from which they have gradually and insensibly sunk again to the lowest state of depravity: and yet these arts have a standard in the remains of antiquity, which music cannot boast. There are classicks in poetry, sculpture, and architecture, which every modern strives to imitate; and he is thought

D

most

moft to excel, who comes neareft to thofe
models. But who will venture to fay, that
the mufician who fhould compofe or perform like Orpheus, or Amphion, would
be defervedly moft applauded now ? Or
who will be bold enough to fay, *how* thefe
immortal bards *did* play and fing, when
not a fingle veftige of their mufic, at
leaft that is intelligible to us, remains ?
As far as we are able to judge, by a com-
parative view of the moft ancient mufic
with the modern, we fhould gain nothing
by imitation. To copy the *canto fermo*
of the Greek church, or that of the
Roman ritual, the moft ancient mufic
now fubfifting, would be to retreat, not
to advance in the fcience of found, or
arts of tafte and expreffion. It would
afford but fmall amufement to ears acquainted with modern harmony, joined
to modern melody. In fhort, to ftop
the world in its motion is no eafy tafk;
on we *muft* go, and he that lags behind

is

Is but lofing time, which it will coft him much labour to recover.

Indeed many of the firft perfons in France, for genius and tafte, give up the point: among whom are Meffieurs Dide-rot, D'Alembert, and the Abbé Arnaud. Meffieurs De la Lande and De Blainville openly rank on the Italian fide likewife; but it feems always with fome degree of referve: (fee M. De la Lande, *Voyage d'un François*, p. 224, tom. vi.) they ftill lay great ftrefs on dancing and decora-tion; but how few fubjects fit for mufic will admit dancing in the texture of the drama? And as to finging and dancing at the fame time, if equally good, they muft diftract and divide the attention in fuch a manner as to make it impoffible to enjoy either: it would be eating of two coftly difhes, or drinking of two ex-quifite wines at once—they reciprocally deftroy the effect of each other. When mufic is really good, and well performed,

the

the hearer of tafte wants no adjunct or additional provocative to ftimulate attention.

Sunday I went to St. Rocque, to hear the celebrated M. Balbaftre, organift of that church, as well as of Notre Dame and the Concert Spirituel *. I had fent the day before to enquire when M. Balbaftre would play, as a ftranger from England was very curious to hear him. He was fo obliging as to fay he fhould be glad to fee me at his houfe, or would attend me at St. Roque, between three and four o'clock.—I preferred the latter, as I thought it would give him leaft trouble, fuppofing he would, of courfe, be at church, but I found he was not expected; and that it was in complaifance that he came. He very politely took me up into the organ-loft with him, where I could fee as well as hear. The organ

* There are four organifts of Notre Dame, who play quarterly — Meffieurs Couperin, Balbaftre, D'Aquin, and Fouquet.

is an immenſe inſtrument, made not above twenty years ago; it has four ſets of keys, with pedals; the great and choir organ communicate by a ſpring: the third row of keys is for the reed ſtops, and the upper for the echoes. This inſtrument has a very good effect below; but above the keys are intolerably noiſy. M. Balbaſtre took a great deal of pains to entertain me; he performed in all ſtyles in accompanying the choir. When the *Magnificat* was ſung, he played likewiſe between each verſe ſeveral minutes, fugues, imitations, and every ſpecies of muſic, even to hunting pieces and jigs, without ſurpriſing or offending the congregation, as far as I was able to diſcover. In *proſing*, I perceived he performed the chant on the pedals, which he doubled with the loweſt part of the left hand, and upon this baſis played with learning and fancy. The baſe part was written in ſemibreves, like our old pſalmody. What

D 3

was

was fung in the choir, without the organ, was inferted in the Gregorian character.

After church M. Balbaftre invited me to his houfe, to fee a fine Rucker harp-fichord which he has had painted infide and out with as much delicacy as the fineft coach or even fnuff-box I ever faw at Paris. On the outfide is the birth of Venus; and on the infide of the cover the ftory of Rameau's moft fa-mous opera, Caftor and Pollux; earth, hell, and elyfium are there reprefented: in elyfium, fitting on a bank, with a lyre in his hand, is that celebrated compofer himfelf; the portrait is very like, for I faw Rameau in 1764. The tone of this inftrument is more delicate than power-ful; one of the unifons is of buff, but very fweet and agreeable; the touch very light, owing to the quilling, which in France is always weak.

M. Balbaftre had in the fame room a very large organ, with pedals, which it

may

may be neceffary for a French organift to have for practice; it is too large and coarfe for a chamber, and the keys are as noify as thofe at St. Roque. However M Balbaftre did his beft to entertain and oblige me, and I had great reafon to be fatisfied both with his politenefs and performance.

Monday 18. This evening I went to St. Gervais, to hear M. Couperin, nephew to the famous Couperin, organift to Louis XIV. and to the regent duke of Orleans, it being the vigil or eve of the Feaft of Dedication, there was a full congregation. I met M. Balbaftre and his family there; and I find this annual feftival is the time for the organifts to difplay their talents. M. Couperin accompanied the *Te Deum,* which was only chanted, with great abilities. The interludes between each verfe were admirable. Great variety of ftops and ftyle, with much learning and knowledge of

the

the inftrument, were fhewn, and a finger
equal in ftrength and rapidity to every
difficulty. Many things of effect were
produced by the two hands, up in the
treble, while the bafe was played on the
pedals.

M. Balbaftre introduced me to M. Couperin, after the fervice was over, and
I was glad to fee two eminent men of
the fame profeffion, fo candid and friendly together. M. Couperin feems to be between forty and fifty; and his tafte is not
quite fo modern, perhaps, as it might be;
but allowance made for his time of life,
for the tafte of his nation, and for the
changes mufic has undergone elfewhere,
fince his youth, he is an excellent organift; brilliant in execution, varied in his
melodies, and mafterly in his modulation.
It is much to be wifhed that fome
opportunity, like this annual meeting,
were given in England to our organifts,
who have talents, and good inftruments
to difplay. It would awaken emulation,

and

and be a ſtimulus to genius; the performer would be ſure of being well
heard, and the congregation well entertained.

- The organ of St. Gervais, which ſeems
to be a very good one, is almoſt new;
it was made by the ſame builder, M. Cli-
quard, as that of St. Rocque. The pedals
have three octaves in compaſs; the tone
of the loud organ is rich, full, and pleaſing,
when the movement is ſlow; but in
quick paſſages, ſuch is the reverberation
in theſe large buildings, every thing is
indiſtinct, and confuſed. Great latitude
is allowed to the performer in theſe interludes; nothing is too light or too grave,
all ſtyles are admitted; and, though M.
Couperin has the true organ touch,
ſmooth and connected; yet he often
tried, and not unſucceſsfully, mere harpſichord paſſages, ſmartly articulated, and
the notes detached and ſeparated.

Tueſday, July 19. Was ſpent in the
king's library.

Wedneſday

Wednesday 20. I heard M. Pagin on the violin, at the house of Mad. Brillon, at Paffy; she is one of the greatest lady-players on the harpsichord in Europe. This lady not only plays the most diffi-cult pieces with great precision, taste, and feeling, but is an excellent fight's-woman; of which I was convinced by her man-ner of executing some of my own music, that I had the honour of presenting to her. She likewise composes; and was so obliging as to play several of her own sonatas, both on the harpsichord and *piano forte,* accompanied on the violin by M. Pagin. But her application and talents are not confined to the harpsi-chord; she plays on several instruments; knows the genius of all that are in com-mon use, which she said it was necessary for her to do, in order to avoid composing for them such things as were either im-practicable or unnatural; she likewise draws well and engraves, and is a most accomplished and agreeable woman. To

this

this lady many of the famous compofers of Italy and Germany, who have refided in France any time, have dedicated their works; among thefe are Schobert and Boccherini.

M, Pagin was a pupil of Tartini, and is regarded here as his beft fcholar; he has a great deal of expreffion and facility of executing difficulties; but whether he did not exert himfelf, as the room was not large, or from whatever caufe it proceeded, I know not, his tone was not powerful. Mufic is now no longer his profeffion; he has a place under the Compte de Clermont, of about two hundred and fifty pounds fterling a year. He had the *honour* of being hiffed at the *Concert Spirituel* for daring to play in the Italian ftyle, and this was the reafon of his quitting the profeffion.

Thurfday. I had the honour of being introduced to the acquaintance of M. L'Abbé Arnaud, of the Academy Royal *des Infcriptions et Belles Lettres*, his converfation

fation confirmed what I had gathered from his writings, that he was not only a man of great learning, but of great tafte. His differtation upon the accents of the Greek tongue is both ingenious and profound ; there is a truth and pre-cifion in his ideas concerning the arts, which are irrefiftible to a mind at all open to conviction. With this gentleman I had the honour to difcufs feveral points relative to the mufic of the ancients, and the happinefs of being confirmed in fome opinions I had already formed, and en-lightened in others.

At the *Comedie Françoife* I was this night very much entertained by the repre-fentation of *La Surprife d'Amour*, and *George Dandin* ; the former is a piece of Marivaux, and was admirably played; the latter is Moliere's, and a mere farce, full of buffoonery and indecency: it is with this piece, as with fome of Shakefpeare's, the name fupports it; for was any modern writer to produce fuch

grofs

grofs ribaldry and nonfenfe, it would be
very fhort lived : at the fame time it
muft be confeffed, that here and there, as
in Shakefpeare's worft pieces, there are
ftrokes of genius and ftrong comic wit
that ought to live for ever. Preville
played admirably a clown's part in both
thefe comedies, his humour is always
eafy and natural, and there is a perpetual
laugh runs through the houfe from the
time he enters, till he quits the ftage. I
perceive that the overtures and act tunes
of this theatre, as of the *Theatre Italien,*
are all either German or Italian ; they
begin to be afhamed of their own mufic
every where but at the ferious opera ; and
this revolution in their fentiments feems
to have been brought about by M. Rouffeau's excellent *Lettre fur la Mufique
Françoife.*

Friday. I met to-day with M. L'Abbé
Rouffier ; had a long converfation with
him relative to ancient mufic ; his
Memoire

Memoire upon that subject, juſt publiſhed, has, gained him great reputation here.
He ſeems to have diſcovered, in the
Triple Progreſſion, 'the true foundation of
all the Greek Syſtems *. I undertook, at
his requeſt, to carry two of his books to
Bologna, one for *Padre Martini,* and one
for the *Inſtitute.*

At dinner to-day I again met with M.
L'Abbé Arnaud , M. Gretry, and the famous Liotard, the painter of Geneva, were
of the party. M. Gretry, the beſt, and, at
preſent, the moſt faſhionable compoſer of
the comic opera, has lived eight years in
Italy, and is author of *Lucile, Le Tableau
parlant,* and the *Huron*; all pieces that have
had great ſucceſs, how deſervedly I do
not pretend to ſay, not having either
heard or ſeen them; but from the eha-
racter given them, by perſons of good
taſte and ſound judgment, I expect them
to be excellent : the author is a young

* Memoire ſur la Muſique des Anciens,
Par s, 1770

7   man,

man, and in appearance and behaviour very agreeable ; he requested me to be the bearer of a letter to *Padre Martini*, under whom he studied some time at Bologna.

It may not be amiss to remark here, that in conversation with M. Gretry, a young Lyric composer, about the poems he had to set, he agreed with me entirely in my assertion, that there were in France, and elsewhere, men, at present, who wrote very pretty verses, full of wit, invention, and passion; admirable to read, but very ill calculated for song; and perhaps one may venture to say, that, among all the ingenious and elegant writers of this age, Metastasio is the best and almost the only *Lyric Poet* *.

A song for music should consist only of one *subject* or *passion*, expressed in as *few*, and as *soft words as possible*. Since the refinement of melody, and the exclusion of recitative, a song, which usually recapitu-

---

* By Lyric Poet is here meant one who writes poems for music

lates,

lates, illustrates, or closes a scene, is not the place for epigrammatic points, or for a number of heterogeneous thoughts and clashing metaphors; if the writer has the least pity for the composer, or love for music, or wishes to afford the least opportunity for symmetry in the air, in his song, I say again, the thought should be *one*, and the expression as easy and laconic as possible: but, in general, every new line in our songs introduces a new thought; so that if the composer is more tender of the poet's reputation than of his own, he must, at every line, change his subject, or be at strife with the poet; and, in either case, the alternative is intolerable.

In an air, it is by reiterated strokes that passion is impressed; and the most passionate of all music is, perhaps, that where a beautiful passage is repeated, and where the first subject is judiciously returned to, while it still vibrates on the ear, and is recent in the memory: this, no doubt,

may

may be, and often is, carried too far; but not by men of true genius and taste.

At night, juſt before my departure from Paris, I went to the Italian theatre, to hear *On ne s'aviſe jamais de tout*, and *Le Huron*. The *Huron* is an entertaining drama, taken from Mr de Voltaire's *Ingenu*; the muſic by M. Gretry, in which there are many pretty and ingenious things, wholly in the *buon guſto* of Italy; which convinced me, that this compoſer had not been eight years in that country for nothing. But I could not help remarking that our young compoſers, who are profeſſed imitators of Italian muſic, though they have never been in Italy, leſs frequently deviate into abſolute Engliſh muſic, than M. Gretry into French; for ſeveral of his melodies are wholly French: but it ſeems not difficult to account for this; in France there are no genuine Italian operas, either ſerious or comic; ſo that England, where we have both in great perfection,

E

in

in the Italian language, compofed and performed by Italians, may be faid to be a better fchool for a young compofer than France; at leaft his tafte, if already formed upon that of Italy, is lefs likely to be vitiated and depraved in a country where good finging may frequently be heard, than in one where it is hardly too much to fay, it is *never* to be heard at the theatres.

LYONS.

From the vicinity of this place to Italy, it was natural to fuppofe that the mufic here would have been tinctured rather more by the Italian *gufto* than at Paris, but, on the contrary, what is bad at Paris, is worfe here. At the theatre, which is a very pretty one, the finging is deteftable: I was entertained however at a coffee-houfe by an Italian family, who, I am certain, were never heard in Italy but in the ftreets, yet here their performance was charming.

The

The father played the firſt violin, and with great ſpirit; the ſecond violin, and the violoncello were played by his two ſons; and the vocal part was performed by his two daughters, who ſung airs and duets by turns. Nothing was demanded by the landlady, but for the coffee and other things that were drank; but the girls, after each ſong, went about the room with a plate, to collect what the generoſity of each new comer would afford, which, I fear, was but little, if one may judge by the attention to the muſic; for ſuch an inceſſant chattering I never heard among the moſt loquacious female goſſips, as the company, not the *audience*, here made, during the prettieſt airs that were either ſung or played.

The firſt violin of this town is an old Venetian, Signor Carminati, one of Tartini's earlieſt ſcholars. And the principal performer on the harpſichord, Signor Léoni; but both have been here long enough to have accommodated them-

ſelves

felves to the mufic and tafte of this country.

I went twice to the cathedral church of St. John, to hear the *Plain Chant à la Romaine*, and found both the church and the mufic as plain and unadorned with pictures, ftatues, harmony, or tafte, as any proteftant church I ever was in. The prebends, who are here called counts, the canons, and twenty-four boys, all fing in unifon, and without organ or books.

GENEVA.

There is but little mufic to be heard in this place, as there is no play-houfe allowed; nor are there organs in the churches, except two, which are ufed for pfalmody only, in the true purity of John Calvin: however, M. Fritz, a good compofer, and excellent performer, on the violin, is ftill living; he has refided here near thirty years, and is well known to all the Englifh lovers of mufic who have vifited Geneva during that time. In his youth he had ftudied under Somis, at Turin.

Turin. It was rather awkward to go to him; but I sent a message over night, and he appointed two o'clock the next day. He lives at a house about a mile out of town. I found him to be a thin, sensible looking old man, and we soon grew very well acquainted. He was so obliging as to play me one of his own solos, which, though extremely difficult, was pleasing, and though he must be near seventy years of age, he still performs with as much spirit as a young man of twenty-five. His bowing and expression are admirable; and he must himself be a *real lover* of music to keep in such high practice, with so few opportunities of displaying his talents, or of receiving their due reward. He is on the point of publishing, by subscription, six symphonies *

Besides M. Fritz, on the practical side, Geneva can boast an excellent theorist,

---

* This excellent performer, when at Paris, some years ago, had the same honours conferred upon him at the *Concert Spirituel* as M. Pugin. (See p 39.)

M. Serre,

M. Serre, an eminent miniature painter, who has written fome learned and ingenious effays on the theory of harmony. I had the pleafure of converfing with him on the fubject, and of communicating to him the plan of my intended hiftory of mufic. He is thought to be very deep in the fcience of found : feemed pleafed with my vifit, and returned it the fame evening; entering very heartily into my views, and feeming folicitous that I fhould purfue them.

My going to M. Fritz, broke into a plan I had formed of vifiting M. de Voltaire at the fame hour, with fome other ftrangers, who were then going to Ferney. But, to fay the truth, befides the vifit to M. Fritz being more *my bufinefs*, I did not much like going with thefe people, who had only a bookfeller to introduce them ; and I had heard that fome Englifh had lately met with a rebuff from M de Voltaire, by going without any letter of recommendation, or any thing

thing to recommend themfelves. He afked them what they wanted? Upon their replying they wifhed only to fee fo extraordinary a man, he faid—" Well, " gentlemen, you now fee me—did you " take me for a wild beaft or monfter, " that was fit only to be ftared at as " a fhow?" This ftory very much frighted me; for not having any intention of going to Geneva, when I left London, or even Paris, I was quite unprovided with a recommendation: however I was determined to fee his place, (which I took to be—

Cette maifon d'Ariflippe, ces jardins d'
 Epicure:

to which he retired in 1755, but was miftaken) I drove to it alone, after I had left M. Fritz. His houfe is three or four miles from Geneva, but near the lake. I approached it with reverence, and a curiofity of the moft minute kind. I enquired *when* I firft trod on his domain; I had an intelligent and talkative

E 4

poftillion, who anfwered all my queftions very fatisfactorily. His eftate is
very large here, and he is building pretty
farm-houfes upon it. He has erected on
the Geneva fide a quadrangular *juftice*, or
gallows, to fhew that he is the *feigneur*.
One of his farms, or rather manufactur-
ing houfes (for he is eftablifhing a manu-
facture upon his eftate) was fo handfome
that I thought it was his *chateau*. We
drove to Ferney, through a charming
country, covered with corn and vines,
in view of the lake and mountains
of Gex, Swifferland, and Savoy. On the
left hand, approaching the houfe, is a neat
chapel with this infcription :

D E O

E R E X I T

V O L T A I R E.

M DCC LXI.*

* When this building was conftructed, M. de
Volta.re gave a curious reafon for placing upon it
this infcription He faid that it was high time to
dedicate *one church to God*, after fo many had been
dedicated to Saints.

I fent

I sent to enquire whether a stranger might be allowed to see the house and gardens, and was answered in the affirmative. A servant soon came, and conducted me into the cabinet or closet where his master had just been writing, which is never shewn when he is at home; but having walked out, I was allowed that privilege. From thence I passed to the library, which is not a very large one, but well filled. Here I found a whole length figure in marble of himself, recumbent, in one of the windows; and many curiosities in another room; a bust of himself, made not two years since; his mother's picture; that of his niece, Mad Denis, his brother, M. Dupuis; the Calas family, and others. It is a very neat and elegant house, not large, or affectedly decorated. I should have said, that close to the chapel, between that and the house, is the theatre, which he built some years ago; where he treated his friends with some of his own tragedies:

it

7

it is now only ufed as a receptacle for wood and lumber, there having been no play acted in it thefe four years. The fervant told me his mafter was feventy-eight, but very well. " *Il travaille,*" faid he " *pendant dix heures chaque jour.*" He ftudies ten hours every day ; writes conftantly without fpectacles, and walks out with only a domeftic, often a mile or two—" *Et le voila, là bas !*"—and fee, yonder where he is.—

He was going to his workmen. My heart leaped at the fight of fo extraordinary a man. He had juft then quitted his garden, and was croffing the court before his houfe. Seeing my chaife, and me on the point of mounting it, he made a fign to his fervant, who had been my *Cicerone,* to go to him, in order, I fuppofe, to enquire who I was. After they had exchanged a few words together, he approached the place where I ftood, motionlefs, in order to contemplate his perfon as much as I could when his eyes were

turned

turned from me; but on feeing him move towards me, I found myfelf drawn by fome irrefiftible power towards him; and, without knowing what I did, I infenfibly met him half way. It is not eafy to conceive it poffible for life to fubfift in a form fo nearly compofed of mere fkin and bone, as that of M. de Voltaire. He complained of decrepitude, and faid he fuppofed I was curious to form an idea of the figure of one walking after death. However his eyes and whole countenance are ftill full of fire; and though fo emaciated, a more lively expreffion cannot be imagined. He enquired after Englifh news, and obferved that poetical fquabbles had given way to political ones; but feemed to think the fpirit of oppofition as neceffary in poetry as in politics. " *Les querelles d'auteurs font pour le bien de la littérature, comme dans un governement libre, les quarelles des grands, et les clameurs des petits font neceffaires*

faires a la liberté." * And added, " When
critics are filent, it does not fo much
prove the age to be correct as dull." He
enquired what poets we had now ; and I
told him we had Mafon and Gray. They
write but little, faid he, and you feem to
have no one who lords it over the reft
like Dryden, Pope, and Swift. I told
him that it was, perhaps, one of the in-
conveniencies of periodical journals, however well executed, that they often
filenced modeft men of genius, while
impudent blockheads were impenetrable,
and unable to feel the critic's fcourge :
that Mr. Gray and Mr Mafon had both
been illiberally treated by mechanical
critics, even in news-papers , and added,
that modefty and love of quiet feemed in
thefe gentlemen to have got the better
even of their love of fame. During this

* Difputes among authors are of ufe to literature ; as the quarrels of the great, and the cla-
mours of the little, in a free government, are neceffary to liberty

con-

converfation, we approached the buildings he was conftructing near the road to
his *chateau*. Thefe, faid he, pointing to
them, are the moft innocent, and, perhaps, the moft ufeful of all my works.
I obferved that he had other works,
which were of far more extenfive ufe,
and would be much more durable than
thofe. He was fo obliging as to fhew me
feveral farm-houfes he had built, and the
plans of others; after which I took my
leave, for fear of breaking in upon his
time, being unwilling to rob the public
of things fo precious as the few remaining moments of this great and univerfal
genius.

T U R I N.

At the firft entrance into Italy, if the
entertainment were as good as at Rome
or Naples, travellers would be inclined
to ftop fhort, but they find the curiofities, both of art and nature, ftill more
numerous and interefting the nearer they
approach thofe capitals.

Turin

Turin is, however, a very beautiful city, though inferior perhaps to many others in antiquities, natural curiosities, and in the number of its artists.

The language here is half French and half Italian, but both corrupted. This cannot be applied to the music, for Turin has produced a Giardini; and there are at present in this city the famous *Dilettante*, Count Benevento, a great performer on the violin, and a good composer; the two Bezozzi's, and Pugnani; all, except the Count, in the service of the King of Sardinia. Their salary is not much above eighty guineas a year each, for attending the chapel royal; but then the service is made very easy to them, as they only perform solos there, and those just when they please. The *Maestro di Capella* is Don Quirico Gasparini. In the chapel there is commonly a symphony played every morning, between eleven and twelve o'clock, by the king's band, which is divided into three orchestras, and

placed

placed in three different galleries; and though far feparated from each other, the performers know their bufinefs fo well that there is no want of a perfon to beat time, as in the opera and *concert fpirituel* at Paris. The king, the royal family, and the whole city feem very conftant in their attendance at mafs; and all their devotion is filently performed at the *Meffa Baffa,* during the fymphony *. On feftivals Signor Pugnani, or the Bezozzis play a folo, and fometimes motets are performed with voices. The organ is in the gallery which faces the king, and in this ftands the principal firft violin.

The ferious opera begins here the fixth of January, the king's name-day, and continues every day, except Friday, till Lent, and this is called the *Carnival.* Here is an excellent tenor voice, Signor

* The morning fervice of the church here is called *Meffa Baffa,* when the prieft performs it in a voice fo little louder than a whifper, that it cannot be heard through the inftruments.

Ottane,

Ottane, who fings with tafte, and in a
pleafing manner. He favoured me with
two or three airs, in different ftyles,
which difcovered him to be a mafter of
his profeffion. He likewife paints well,
in the manner of Claude Lorrain and Du
Vernet, and is fometimes employed as a
painter by his Sardinian majefty. In
October a company of burletta performers
comes hither, and remains till Chriftmas,
at the little theatre, where there is,
during fummer, a company of *buffo* come-
dians, which exhibits every night, except
Friday, *una farfa fatta da ridere,* and an
intermezzo in mufica a quattro voci. *
This continues till the burlettas begin.
I went thither the evening after my arrival; there was not much company;
the boxes, or *palchetti,* are all engaged by
the year, fo that ftrangers have no place
but in the pit; which, however, is far
more comfortable than the *parterre* or

* A farce to laugh at, and a mufical interlude
for four voices.

pit,

pit, at Paris, where the company ftand the whole time; and even than that at London, where they are much crowded; but there are backs to the benches in this theatre, which are of double ufe, as they keep off the crowd behind, and fupport thofe who fill them. This theatre is not fo large as that at Lyons, but pretty, and capable of holding much company: it is *diflungato*, or of an oblong form, with the corners rounded off. There are no galleries in it, but then there are five rows of boxes, one above another, twenty-four in each row; and each box will contain fix perfons, amounting in all to feven hundred and twenty; there is one ftage-box only on each fide. The farce was truly what it promifed, except the laughing part, as it did not produce that effect. The *intermezzo* was not bad; the mufic pretty, but old; the finging very indifferent for Italy, though it would have been very good in France. However, it is but juft to fay, that, as a

F   drama,

drama, the French comic operas have greatly the advantage over the Italian; take away the muſic from the French, and they would be ſtill pretty comedies; but, without muſic, the Italian would be inſupportable. There were four characters; the two girls were juſt not offenſive. Of the men ſo much cannot be ſaid: none of them would have pleaſed in London; and the Italians themſelves hold theſe performances in no very high eſtimation: they talk the whole time, and ſeldom attend to any thing but one or two favourite airs, during the whole piece: * the only two that were applauded were encored; and I obſerved, that the performer does not take it as ſuch a great favour to be applauded here as in England, where, whenever a hand is moved, all illuſion is deſtroyed by a bow or a

* I ſhall have frequent occaſion to mention the noiſe and inattention at the muſical exhibitions in Italy, but muſic there is cheap and common, whereas in England it is a coſtly exotic, and more highly prized.

curtſey

curtfey from the performer, who is a
king, a queen, or fome great perfonage,
ufually going off the ftage in diftrefs, or
during the emotions of fome ftrong paffion. If Mr. Garrick, in fome of his
principal characters, was to fubmit to
fuch a humiliating practice, it would furely be at the expence of the audience, who
would every inftant be told, that it was
not Lear, Richard, or Macbeth they faw
before them, but Mr. Garrick.

Friday 1 3 This morning I vifited the two
Signor Bezozzis, whofe talents are well
known to all travellers of tafte in mufic.
Their long and uninterrupted regard for
each other is as remarkable as their performance. They are brothers; the eldeft
feventy, and the youngeft upwards of
fixty. They have fo much of the *Idem
velle et idem nolle* about them, that they
have ever lived together in the utmoft
harmony and affection, carrying their
fimilarity of tafte to their very drefs,

which

which is the fame in every particular,
even to buttons and buckles. They are
batchelors, and have lived fo long, and in
fo friendly a manner together, that it is
thought here, whenever one of them dies,
the other will not long furvive him. My
introduction to thefe eminent performers
was eafy and agreeable, having been favoured with a letter to them from Mr.
Giardini, who had been fo kind as to fave
me the confufion of afking them to play
upon fo fhort an acquaintance, by telling
them, in his letter, how much they would
oblige me by fuch a favour. The eldeft
plays the hautbois, and the youngeft the
baffoon, which inftrument continues the
fcale of the hautbois, and is its true bafe.
Their compofitions generally confift of
felect and detached paffages, yet fo elabo-
rately finifhed, that, like felect thoughts
or maxims in literature, each is not a frag-
ment, but a whole : thefe pieces are in a
peculiar manner adapted to difplay the
powers of the performers ; but it is difficult

cult to defcribe their ftile of playing.
Their compofitions, when printed, give
but an imperfect idea of it. So much
expreffion ! fuch delicacy ! fuch a perfect
acquiefcence and agreement together,
that many of the paffages feem heart-felt
fighs, breathed through the fame reed.
No brilliancy of execution is aimed at,
all are notes of meaning. The imitations
are exact ; the melody is pretty equally
diftributed between the two inftruments ;
each *forte, piano, crefcendo, diminuendo,*
and *appoggiatura,* is obferved with a
minute exactnefs, which could be at-
tained only by fuch a long refidence and
ftudy together. The eldeft has loft his
under front teeth, and complained of age;
and it is natural to fuppofe that the performance of each has been better : however, to me, who heard them now for the
firft time, it was charming. If there
is any defect in fo exquifite a performance,
ance, it arifes from the *equal perfection*
of the *two parts;* which diftracts the

F 3 atten-

attention, and renders it impoffible to liften to both, when both have diffimilar melodies equally pleafing.

They were born at Parma, and have been upwards of forty years in the fervice of his Sardinian majefty, without ever quitting Italy, except in one fhort excurfion to Paris, or even Turin, but for that journey, and one to vifit the place of their nativity. They are fober, regular perfons, and are in eafy circumftances; have a town and country houfe, in the former are many good pictures, particularly one of Lodovico Carrach, fuperior to every picture I had feen by that mafter.

After this vifit I heard a full piece performed at the king's chapel, and then went to fee the great opera-houfe, which is reckoned one of the fineft in Europe. It is very large and elegant; the machinery and decorations are magnificent, I was carried into every part of it, even to the taylor's work-fhop. Here are fix rows of boxes above the pit, both larger and

deeper

deeper than thofe of the other theatre: the king is at the chief expence of this opera. Thofe who have boxes for the feafon, pay, in a kind of fees only, two or three guineas; money at the door being only taken for fitting in the pit.

The itinerant muficians, *Anglicè*, ballad-fingers, and fidlers, at Turin perform in concert. A band of this kind came to the *Hôtel, la bonne femme*, confifting of two voices, two violins, a guitar, and bafe, bad enough indeed, though far above our fcrapers. The fingers, who were girls, fung duets very well in tune, accompanied by the whole band. The fame people at night performed on a ftage in the *grand place* or fquare, where they fold their ballads as our quack doctors do their noftrums, but with far lefs injury to fociety. In another part of the fquare, on a different ftage, a man and woman fung Venetian ballads, in two parts, very agreeably, accompanied by a dulcimer.

Saturday

Saturday 14. Signor Pugnani played a concerto this morning at the king's chapel, which was crowded on the occasion. It is an elegant rotund, built of black marble, and happily conftructed for mufic, being very high, and terminated by a dome. I need fay nothing of the performance of Signor Pugnani, his talents being too well known in England to require it. I fhall only obferve, that he did not appear to exert himfelf; and it is not to be wondered at, as neither his Sardinian majefty, nor any one of the numerous royal family, feem to pay much attention to mufic. There is a gloomy famenefs at this court, in the daily repetition of ftate parade and prayer.

Signor Baretti, of this place, in confequence of a letter from his brother in London, received me very politely, and took great pains to be ufeful to me while I remained in Turin; and in this he fucceeded very much, by introducing me to

Padre

Padre Beccaria, for whom, at first sight, I conceived the highest regard and veneration.

He is not above forty; with a large and noble figure, he has something open, natural, intelligent, and benevolent in his countenance, that immediately captivates. We had much conversation concerning electricity, Dr. Franklin, Dr. Priestly, and others. He was pleased to make me a present, finding me an *amateur,* (which should be always translated a *dabler)* of his last book *, and the syllabus of the *Memoire* he lately sent to our Royal Society. He likewise wrote in my tablets a recommendatory note to M. Laura Bassi, the famous *dottoreffa* and academist at Bologna ; recommended to me some books, and was so kind, and with a manner so truly simple, that I shall for ever remember this visit with pleasure. Mr. Martin,

---

* *Experimenta, atque Obferuationes, quibus Electricitas vindex late conflituitur atque explicatur.* Taurin. 1769.

the

the banker here, came after me to Signor
Beccaria's; and this great mathematician
is so little acquainted with worldly concerns, especially money-matters, that he
was quite astonished and pleased at the
ingenuity and novelty of a letter of credit.
Mr. Martin desiring to look at mine, in
his presence, in order to know how he
might send my letters after me, the good
father could hardly comprehend how this
letter could be *argent comptant*, ready
money, throughout Italy.

He charged me with compliments to
Padre Boscovich at Milan, and *Padre Martini* at Bologna; and I left my new acquaintance, impressed with the highest
respect and affection for him. I must just
mention one particular more relative to
this great and good man, which I had
from Signor Baretti; that he, through
choice, lives up six pair of stairs, among
his observatories, machines, and mathematical instruments; and there does every
thing for himself, even to making his bed,
and dressing his dinner. I visit-

I vifited the univerfity, or royal library, where there are fifty thoufand volumes, and many manufcripts, the catalogue of which fills two volumes in folio. The accefs to thefe books is eafy, both before and after dinner, every day, holidays excepted. I was very politely treated there, on Signor Baretti's account, by Signor Grela, the diftributer of the books, who fhewed me feveral of the moft ancient MSS.

Among my mufical enquiries at Turin, David Rizio was not forgotten; who having been a native of this city, and his father a mufician here, I thought it likely, if I could find any mufic compofed by either of them, or by their cotemporaries, that it would determine the long difputed queftion, whether David Rizio was author of the Scots melodies attributed to him *.

* The iffue of this enquiry will be related in the Hiftory of Mufic.

In

In my journey from Turin to Milan, I ſtopped a little while at Vercelli; which is a large town, ſaid to contain twenty thouſand inhabitants; where I met with a book on the ſubject of muſic, and with its author, Signor Carlo Geo. Teſtori, with whom I had the pleaſure of converſing.

MILAN.

In this city, which is very large and populous, muſic is much cultivated. Signor Battiſta San Martini is organiſt of two or three churches here; I had a letter to him from Signor Giardini, which procured me a very agreeable reception. He is brother to the famous Martini of London, who ſo long delighted us with his performance on the hautbois, as well as by his compoſitions. The muſic of Signor Battiſta San Martini of Milan is well known in England.

But what I was moſt curious after here, was the Ambroſian Chant or church ſer-

vice,

vice, which is peculiar to Milan, after the manner inſtituted by St. Ambroſe, two hundred years before the Roman, or that of St. Gregory.

At the *Duomo*, or great church, which, in ſize, is ſuperior to every Gothic ſtructure in Italy, and ſaid to be nearly as big as St. Peter's at Rome, there are two large organs, one on each ſide the choir. On feſtivals there are oratorios, *a due cori*, for two choirs, and then both organs are uſed ; on common days only one. There are two organiſts ; Signor J. Bach, before his arrival in England, was one of them: at preſent the firſt organiſt is Signor G. Corbeli ; he is reckoned a very able man in his profeſſion, I heard him play ſeveral times, in a maſterly grave ſtile, ſuited to the place and inſtrument.

Friday, July 17. After hearing the ſervice chanted in the Ambroſian manner, peculiar to this place, I was introduced to Signor Jean Andre Fioroni, *Maeſtro di Ca-*
pella

pella at the great church, who invited me into the orcheftra, fhewed me the fervices they were juft going to fing, printed on wood, in four parts, the *cantus* and *tenor* on the left fide, and *altus et baffus* on the right, without bars. Out of this one book, after the tone was given by the organift, the whole four parts were fung without the organ. There was one boy, and three *caftrati* for the *foprano* and *contr' alto* with two tenors and two bafes, under the direction of Signor Fioroni, who beat the time, and now and then fung. Thefe fervices were compofed about one hundred and fifty years ago, by a Maeftro di Capella of the *Duomo*, and are much in the ftile of our fervices of that time, confifting of good harmony, ingenious points and contrivances, but no melody. From hence I went home with Signor Fioroni, who was fo obliging as to fhew me all his mufical curiofities, (he had before done me the favour to fhew me thofe in the *Sacrifti)* and played over and fung to me

me a whole oratorio of his own compôfi-
tion He likewife favoured me with a copy
of one of his own fervices, in eight parts
in fcore, for two choirs, which I begged
cf him, in order to convince the world,
that, though the theatrical ftile and that
of the church are now much the fame,
when inftruments and additional fingers
are employed, yet the ancient grave ftile
is not wholly loft *.

Piccini had been at Milan this year,
during the carnival, for which he compofed a ferious opera. The principal
fingers were, firft man, Signor Aprile;
firft woman, la Signora Piccinelli; and
the two principal dancers were M. and
Mad Pique.

After the carnival he compofed a burletta, called *Il Regno nella Luna*, for the
performers, who are ftill here. Piccini
had been gone from hence but a little
while before my arrival.

* This piece, with feveral other curious compofitions, mentioned hereafter, will be publifhed.

There

There is no serious opera at Milan but in carnival time. The first burletta I heard there, was *L'Amore Artegiano;* it began at eight, and was not over till twelve o'clock. the music, which had pretty things in it, was by Signor Floriano Gafman, in the service of the emperor, who played the harpfichord. There were in it seven characters, all pretty well done, but no one *very* well, as to singing.

The dance in this opera was very entertaining; there was an infinite number of principals and figurers employed in it, besides two *faltatori,* Signor and Signora Palecini, who gained more applause than all the rest; indeed their activity was very surprising: there were two others, who danced *all Inglefe,* and there was a French *peruquier* in this burletta, whose finging was to be French: but their imitations here are such as ours in London, when we are to take off the Italians; that is to say, about as like as a miferable fign-poft, called the King or Queen's head, usually is to George the
Third,

Third, or Queen Charlotte : one is more inclined to laugh *at* than *with* such mimies. In this dance the ftage was illuminated in a moft fplendid, and, to me, new manner, with *lampioni coloriti*, or coloured lamps, which had a very pretty effect; the front fcene and ceiling, as well as the fides, had an infinite number of thefe lamps.

The theatre here is very large and fplendid; it has five rows of boxes on each fide, one hundred in each row; and parallel to thefe runs a broad gallery, round the houfe, as an avenue to every row of boxes : each box will contain fix perfons, who fit at the fides, facing each other. Acrofs the gallery of communication is a complete room to every box, with a fireplace in it, and all conveniences for refrefhments and cards. In the fourth row is a *pharo* table, on each fide the houfe, which is ufed during the performance of the opera. There is in front a very large box, as big as a common London dining-

G   room,

room, set apart for the Duke of Modena, governor of Milan, and the *Principessina* his daughter, who were both there. The noise here during the performance was abominable, except while two or three airs and a duet were singing, with which every one was in raptures : at the end of the duet, the applause continued with unremitting violence till the performers returned to sing it again, which is here the way of encoring a favourite air. The first violin was played by Lucchini : the band is very numerous, and orchestra large in proportion to the size of the theatre, which is much bigger than the great opera-house at Turin. In the highest story the people sit in front ; and those for whom there are no seats, stand behind in the gallery : all the boxes here are appropriated for the season, as at Turin. Between the acts the company from the pit come up stairs, and walk about the galleries. There was only one dance, but that very long.

It

It is not the Englifh genius to be
fatisfied with their prefent condition
or pòffeffions, or elfe, upon the whole,
one may venture to pronounce, that fuch
a comic opera as that of laft winter in
London, might have contented them;
which, on the fide of finging, was greatly fuperior to this; nor did I meet,
throughout Italy, with three fuch performers at leaft on the fame ftage, as
Signor Lovatini, Signor Morigi, and
Signora Guadagni.

The opera here is carried on by thirty
noblemen, who fubfcribe fixty zechins
each, for which every fubfcriber has a
box*; the reft of the boxes are let for
the year at fifty zechins *la prima fila*, or
firft row, forty the fecond, thirty the
third, and in proportion for the reft. The
chance money only arifes from the pit and
upper feats, or *picconai:* they perform
every night except Fridays.

* A zechin is a gold coin, current all over
Italy, equal in value to about nine fhillings
Englifh.

Wednefday

Wednefday 18. I went this morning, for the firft time, to the Ambrofian Library, which, in fize, appears but diminutive, after reading the accounts given of it in books of travels, and after having feen the *Biblioteque du Roi* at Paris, which is, at leaft, ten times as big; there is, in fact, but one large room filled with printed books, and two fmall ones for French literature, printed and MS. then a room full of copies only of the beft ancient ftatues at Rome and Florence, and, laftly, a large hall or faloon, full indeed of wonderful performances of the greateft painters; among thefe are many ineftimable works of Leonardo da Vinci, and Jean Breugel, of Antwerp, the high finifher, whofe four elements in this collection are faid to have coft him his fight. There is an admirable portrait in the collection, by this painter, of the organift Merula *. Upon

* Claudius Merulus, as the Germans called him, was of Antwerp, and flourifhed in the fixteenth century.

my

my enquiring for the catalogue of MSS. I was told it was not ufual to fhew it, but I might fee any one in the collection, if I would afk for it by name, but I knew no more the name than the contents: I was in queft of new exiftences, new literary beings, unpolluted by profane compilers and printers. Upon explaining my errand to Milan, and faying it was chiefly to afcertain the time of eftablifhing the Ambrofian Chant in that church, I was told that *Padre Martini* had made the fame enquiries, but without fuccefs; it feeming as if that chant had been given to St. Ambrofe by the writers of his life, one after the other, without fufficient proof. This was rather difcouraging, however I did not, as yet, give up the point, and I afterwards found more favour in the fight of the librarians. As yet I had not delivered my letters to thofe perfons, whofe countenance, in my future vifits, procured me every fatisfaction this library could afford.

G 3

A gen-

A gentleman of Parma, with whom, I had travelled from Paris, having a letter from M. Meffier to Padre Bofcovich, giving him an account of a new comet which he had difcovered on the eleventh of June, I had the pleafure of accompanying my friend in his vifit to this father at the Jefuits College, who received us both with great courtefy; and being told that I was an Englifhman, a lover of the fciences, and ambitious of feeing fo celebrated a man, he addreffed himfelf to me in a particular manner. He had feveral young ftudents of quality with him, and faid he expected that morning three perfons of diftinction to fee his inftruments, and invited me to be of the party; I gladly accepted the propofal, and he immediately began to fhew and explain to me feveral machines and contrivances which he had invented for making optical experiments, before the arrival of the *Signori*, who were a Knight of Malta, a nephew of Pope Benedict XIV. and

another

another *Cavaliere*. He then went on, and furprifed and delighted us all very much, particularly with his *Stet Sol*, by which he can fix the fun's rays, paffing through an aperture or a prifm, to any part of the oppofite wall he pleafes : he likewife feparates and fixes any of the prifmatic colours of the rays. Shewed us a method of forming an aquatic prifm, and the effects of joining different lenfes, all extremely plain and ingenious. He has publifhed a Latin differtation on thefe matters at Vienna. Then we afcended to different obfervatories; where I found his inftruments mounted in fo ingenious and fo convenient a manner, as to give me the utmoft pleafure. He was fo polite as to addrefs himfelf to me always in French, as I had at firft accofted him in that language, and in which I was at this time much more at my eafe than in Italian. M. Meffier had told him the comet had very little motion, being almoft ftationary; but Padre Bofcovich

after-

afterwards found it fo rapid as to move fifty degrees in a day. *Mais la comete, Monfieur, lui dis-je, ou eft elle a prefent? Avec le foleil, elle eft mariée.* The late Duke of York made him a prefent of one of Short's twelve-inch reflectors, of twenty guineas price; but he has an acromatic one, by the fame maker, which coft one hundred. The expence of his obfervatory, which is defrayed by himfelf, muft have been enormous. He is univerfity profeffor at Pavia, where he fpends his winters. If any new difcoveries are to be made in aftronomy, they may be expected from this learned Jefuit; whofe attention to optical experiments for the improvement of glaffes, upon which fo much depends; and whofe great number of admirable inftruments of all forts, joined to the excellence of the climate, and the wonderful fagacity he has difcovered in the conftruction of his obfervatory and machines, form a concurrence of favourable circumftances, not

easily

eafily to be found elfewhere. He complained very much of the filence of the Englifh aftronomers, who anfwer none of his letters. He was feven months in England, and during that time was very much with Mr. Mafkaline, Dr. Shepherd, Dr. Bevis, and Dr. Maty, with whom he hoped to keep up a correfpondence. He had, indeed, lately received from Mr. Profeffor Mafkaline the laft Nautical Almanack, with Mayer's Lunar Tables, who gave him hopes of reviving their literary intercourfe. He is a tall, ftrong built man, upwards of fifty, of a very agreeable addrefs. He was refufed admiffion into the French academy, when at Paris, though a member, by the parliament, on account of his being a Jefuit: but if all Jefuits were like this father, making ufe only of fuperior learning and intellects for the advancement of fcience, and the happinefs of mankind, one would have wifhed this fociety to be as durable as the world. As it is, it feems as if

equity

equity required that fome difcrimination
fhould be made in condemning the Jefuits; for though good policy may' require a diffolution of their order, yet humanity certainly makes one wifh 'to pre-
ferve the old, the infirm, and the innocent, from the general wreck and deftruc-
tion due only to the guilty.

The fecond opera I heard 'here was
La Lavandara Aftuta, a *Pafticcio*, with 'a
large portion of Piccini's airs in it. Gari-
baldi, the firft man, had a better part in
this burletta than in the firft, and fung
very well. He has a pleafing voice, and
much tafte and expreffion; was encored,
alla Italiana, two or three times. One of
the *Baglioni* * fings better than the two
others, and had more to do. Caratoli
diverted the people at Milan very much by
his action and humour, though local, and
what would not pleafe in England: the

* There are fix fifters of that name, all fingers,
three of them were at Milan 'tis a Bolognefe
family.

dance

dance was the fame as that I had feen before.

A private concert in Italy is called an, *accademia*; the firft I went to was compofed entirely of *dilettanti*; *il padrone*, or the mafter of the houfe, played the firft violin, and had a very powerful hand; there were twelve or fourteen performers, among whom were feveral good violins; there were likewife two German flutes, a violoncello, and fmall double bafe; they executed, reafonably well, feveral of our Bach's fymphonies, different from thofe printed in England: all the mufic here is in MS. But what I liked moft was the vocal part by *La Signora Padrona della Cafa*, or lady of the houfe, fhe had an agreeable well-toned voice, a good fhake, the right fort of tafte and expreffion, and fung (fitting down, with the paper on the common inftrumental defk) wholly without affectation, feveral pretty airs of Traetta.

Upon

Upon the whole, this concert was much upon a level with our own private concerts among gentlemen in England, the performers were fometimes in and fometimes out; in general, however, the mufic was rather better chofen, the execution more brilliant and full of fire, and the finging much nearer perfection than we can often boaft on fuch occafions; not, indeed, in point of voice or execution, for in refpect to them our females are, at leaft, equal to our neighbours, but in the *portamento* or direction of the voice, in expreffion and in difcretion *.

---

* It is humbly hoped that my fair countrywomen will not take offence at the ufe of the word *difcretion*, as its acceptation here is wholly confined to mufic, in which the love for what is commonly called *gracing*, is carried to fuch a pitch of *indifcretion*, as frequently to change paffages from good to bad, and from bad to worfe. A *little* paint may embellifh an ordinary face, though a great deal would render it hideous, but true beauty is furely beft in its natural ftate.

The

The fame day, Friday, July 20, there was mufic at three different churches; I wifhed to be at them all during the performances, but it was impoffible to be prefent at more than two of them; the firft of which was in the morning, at the church of *Santa Maria Secreta*; it was a *Meffa in mufica*, by Signor Monza, and under his direction: his brother played the principal violoncello, with much facility of execution, but neither in tone or tafte very pleafing. The firft violin was played by Signor Lucchini, who leads at the burletta; there were two or three *caftrati* among the fingers. A little paltry organ was erected on the occafion; there was a large one in the church, but it ftood in a gallery, which was too fmall for a band: the mufic was pretty; long and ingenious introductory fymphonies to each *concento*, as each part or divifion of the mafs is called; and the whole was in good tafte, and fpirited, but the organ, hautbois, and fome of the fiddles being bad, deftroyed the effect of feveral things that

were

were well defigned. As a principal violin, Signor Lucchini is not of the firft clafs ; there is no want of hand, but great want of finifhing : he had feveral folo parts given him, and made three or four clofes

The finging, though in general rather better than at our oratorios, was by no means fo good as we often hear in England at the Italian opera. As yet I had met with no *great* finger fince my arrival in Italy. The firft *foprano* here was what we fhould call in England a pretty good finger, with a pretty good voice , his tafte neither original nor fuperior. The fecond finger, a *contr' alto,* had likewife but a moderate portion of merit; though his voice was pleafing, and he never gave offence by the injudicious ufe of it. But,

> " 'Tis in *fong* as it 'tis in painting,
> Much may be right, yet much be wanting."

However, fuch a performance as this fhould not be criticifed too feverely, for

it

it is heard for nothing. I speak as a traveller; but the people of Italy, who contribute so much to the support of the church, are surely well entitled to have these treats excellent.

The second mass I heard to-day was composed by Battista San Martini, and performed under his direction at the church of the Carmini; the symphonies were very ingenious, and full of the spirit and fire peculiar to that author. The instrumental parts in his compositions are well written; he lets none of the performers be long idle; and the violins, especially, are never suffered to sleep. It might, however, sometimes be wished that he would ride his *Pegafus* with a curb-bridle; for he seems absolutely to run away with him. Without metaphor, his music would please more if there were fewer notes, and fewer *allegros* in it : but the impetuosity of his genius impels him to run on in a succession of rapid movements, which in the end fatigue both the performer and the

8   hearers.

hearers. Marchefini, whom I did not much like, fung the firft *faprano* part; Ciprandi, an excellent tenor, who was in England a few years ago, and whofe caft of parts has never fince been fo well filled, fung here in a manner far fuperior to all the reft. The band was but indifferent; the firft violin was played by Zuccherini, who is reckoned here a good mufician. I find performances of this kind but ill attended, no people of fafhion are ever feen at them; the congregation feems to confift principally of the clergy, trades-people, mechanics, country clowns, and beggars, who are, for the moft part, very inattentive and reftlefs, feldom remaining in the church during the whole performance. San Martini is *Maeftro di Capella* to half the churches in Milan, and the number of maffes he has compofed is almoft infinite; however his fire and invention ftill remain in their utmoft vigour.

At

At another church vefpers were performed this evening by Monks and Nuns only; I was too late in my attempt to hear them : however I was carried to one of the largeft *accademia* of Milan, where there were upwards of thirty performers, and among them feveral good ones. Madame Dé fung; and though fhe had a cold, which affected her voice, did feveral things which difcovered her to have the abilities of a capital finger. Befides two fongs of great compafs and execution, fhe fung an *adagio* with infinite tafte. The mafter at the harpfichord was Signor Scotti, two or three of Mr. Bach's overtures were played, and very much approved; and an excellent one of Martini, with a duet violin concerto of Raymond, a German, very well written, and, though difficult, well performed, by two violins of different powers, but both good in their way; one an elderly man, with great neatnefs and delicacy of tone, but feeble; the other very young, with a

H force

force and fire which will foon render him
a very great player; efpecially as to thefe
requifites he joins expreffion : it was an
admirable conteft between age and youth,
judgment and genius. Thefe were all
virtuofi or profeffors, the reft of the band
was made up of *dilettanti*.

Saturday 21   It did not feem foreign
to my bufinefs in Italy to vifit the *Palazzo
Simonetto*, a mile or two from Milan, to
hear the famous echo, about which travellers have faid fo much, that I rather
fufpected exaggeration. This is not the
place to enter deeply into the doctrine of
reverberation ; I fhall referve the attempt
for another work ; as to the matter of
fact, this echo is very wonderful. The
Simonetto palace is near no other building ; the country all around is a dead flat,
and no mountains are nearer than thofe of
Swifferland, which are upwards of thirty
miles off. This palace is now uninha-
bited and in ruin, but has been pretty ;
the front is open, and fupported by very
                                    light

light double Ionic pillars, but the echo is only to be heard behind the house, which, next to the garden has two wings.

Front

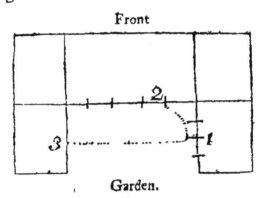

Garden.

1. The best window to make the experiment at.

2. The best window to hear the echo from.

3. A dead wall with only windows painted upon it, from whence the repetitions seem to proceed.

Now, though it is natural to suppose that the opposite walls reflect the sound, it is not easy to say in what manner, as the form of the building is a very common one, and no other of the same construc-

tion,

tion, that I have ever heard of, produces the fame effects. I made experiments of all kinds, and in every fituation, with the voice, flow, quick, with a trumpet, which a fervant who was with me founded; with a piftol, and a mufquet, and always found agreeable to the doctrine of echos, that the more quick and violent the percuffion of the air, the more numerous were the repetitions; which, upon firing the mufquet, amounted to upwards of fifty, of which the ftrength feemed regularly to diminifh, and the diftance to become more remote. Such a mufical canon might be contrived for one fine voice here, according to father Kircher's method, as would have all the effect of two, three, and even four voices. One blow of a hammer produced a very good imitation of an ingenious and practifed footman's knock at a London door, on a vifiting night. A fingle *ha!* became a long horfe-laugh; and a forced note, or a found overblown in the trumpet, became

the

the moſt ridiculous and laughable noiſe imaginable.

The compoſers to be found in this city are innumerable. I was carried to-day to hear three ladies ſing, who are ſiſters, and I found at their houſe Signor Lampugnani, who is their maſter: he lives conſtantly at Milao, plays the firſt harpſichord at the opera, in the abſence of the compoſers, and puts together the *paſticcios* Theſe ladies did him great credit, by the manner in which they ſung ſeveral ſongs, duets, and trios. One of them performed a long ſcene in the *Olimpiade* of Jomelli, which is extremely difficult; the compoſition is juſtly admired for the boldneſs and learning in the modulation, which is *recherchée*, but expreſſive and pleaſing: I have procured a copy of this ſcene. There was at the ſame houſe a good performer on the violin, Signor Paſqualini, who accompanied the ſongs with great neatneſs and judgment.

H 3 After

After this I went to the opera-houfe;
where the audience was very much difappointed; the firft tenor, and only good
finger in it, being ill. All his part was
cut out, and the *Baritono*, in the character
of a bluftering old father, who was to
abufe his fon violently in the firft fcene
and fong, finding he had no fon there,
gave a turn to the misfortune, which diverted the audience very much, and made
them fubmit to their difappointment with
a better grace than they would have done
in England; for inftead of his fon, he
fell foul on the prompter, who here, as at
the opera in England, pops his head out
of a little trap-door on the ftage. The
audience were fo delighted with this at-
tack upon the prompter, who is ever regarded as an enemy to their pleafures,
that they encored the fong in which it
was made. However, after the firft act
and the dance, I came away, as the lights
at the opera-houfe here affected my eyes
in a very painful manner; and there being

no

no retribution for this suffering to-night, I denied myself the rest of the performance.

Sunday 22. This morning, after hearing the Ambrosian service in all its perfection, at the *Duomo*, I went to the Convent of *Santa Maria Maddalena*; I heard several motets performed by the nuns; it was their feast-day. The composition was by Signor B. S. Martini, who is *Maestro di Capella*, and teaches to sing at this convent. He made me ample amends for the want of flow movements in his mass on Friday, by an *adagio* in the motet of to-day, which was truly divine, and divinely sung by one of the sisters, accompanied, on the organ only, by another. It was by far the best singing, in every respect, I had heard since my arrival in Italy; where there is so much, that one soon grows fastidious. At my first coming I both hungered and thirsted after music, but I now had had

H 4 almost

almoft my fill; and we are more fevere critics upon a full ftomach, than with a good appetite. Several of the nuns fung, fome but indifferently, but one of them had an excellent voice; full, rich, fweet, and flexible, with a true fhake, and exquifite expreffion; it was delightful, and left nothing to wifh, but duration!

There is a general complaint in England againft loud accompaniments; and if an evil there, it is doubly fuch in Italy. In the opera-houfe nothing but the inftruments can be heard, unlefs when the *baritoni* or bafe voices fing, who can contend with them, nothing but noife can be heard through noife; a delicate voice is fuffocated: it feems to me as if the orcheftra not only played too loud, but had too much to do.

Befides the organ in this convent for the choruffes, there was an organ and harpfichord together, which was likewife played by one of the nuns; and the accompaniment of that inftrument alone with

with the heavenly voice abovementioned, pleafed me beyond defcription, and not fo much by what it *did*, as by what it did *not* do; furely one cannot hear too much of fuch a mellifluous voice. All the jargon of different parts, of laboured contrivance, and difficult execution, is little better than an ugly mafk upon a beautiful face; even harmony itfelf, upon fuch occafions is an evil, when it becomes a fovereign inftead of a fubject. I know this is not fpeaking like a *mufician*, but I fhall always give up the *profeffion*, when it inclines to pedantry; and give way to my feelings, when they feem to have reafon on their fide. If a voice be coarfe, or otherwife difpleafing, the lefs it is heard the better, and then tumultuous accompaniments and artful contrivances may have their ufe; but a fingle note from fuch a voice as that I heard this morning, penetrates deeper into the foul, than the fame note from the moft perfect inftrument upon earth can do, which,

at

at heft, is but an imitation of the human voice.

The mufic this morning was entirely performed by the nuns themfelves, who were invifible to the congregation; and though the church of the convent is open to the public, like a common parifh church, in which the priefts are in fight, as elfewhere, yet the refponfes are made behind the altar, where the organ is placed. I looked in vain for that and the fingers, upon my firft entrance into the church, without knowing it belonged to a convent. Upon my praifing this fing-ing, I was told that there were feveral convents here in which the nuns fing much better. Of this I muft own I was in doubt; I could only fay I fhould be very glad to hear them. And I was fo pleafed with this finging, that though I dined with a private family, in a very fó-ciable and agreeable way, I ran from the company ere the fecond courfe was ferved, in hopes of hearing more of it at

the

the fame convent ; and was fo fortunate
as to enter it juft as the fervice was begun, and heard the fame motet repeated
again by the fame nun, and with double
delight.

The ballad-fingers at Milan fing duets
in the ftreets, fometimes with, and fometimes without inftruments, and keep very
firm to their parts ; but I did not perceive that they mount a ftage here as at
Turin.

At night, the firft tenor of the burletta continuing to be ill, there was an
accademia at the theatre, inftead of an
opera. The fingers were the fame that I
had heard before ; they were placed on
the ftage in much the fame manner as at
the annual performance in London for
the benefit of decayed muficians : they
fat at tables, two and two, and when they
fung, each got up, and advanced towards
the audience. There were feveral opera
overtures performed, but no folos ; inftead
of them there were dances between the

acts of the concert. On the stage, behind the singers, which were six, there stood six servants the whole time. The *Baglioni* appeared to more advantage to-night than in the opera, especially Clementina, who, in a less theatre, would be a very agreeable singer; in this all voices are lost.

Monday 23. This morning I went early with father Moiana, a very agreeable Dominican, to the Ambrosian Library, and with some difficulty got a sight of two or three very ancient manuscripts relative to my purpose, and of the pompous edition of the services performed at the Duomo, printed in four vast volumes in folio, 1619, for the use of that church only. The printing is very neat, upon wood, but without bars, and consequently not in score, though the parts are all in sight, upon opposite pages, *soprano* and *tenor* on the first, and *alto* and *basso* on the second page : I made several extracts

from

from all thefe. Signor Oltrocchi, the librarian, began to be more communicative than at firft. One of the moft ancient books he fhewed me this morning, was a beautiful manufcript of the ninth century, and well preferved. It is a miffal, written before the time of Guido, at leaft two hundred years, and confequently before the lines ufed by that monk were invented. The notes are little more than accents of different kinds put over the hymns *. I met with a noble and learned churchman here, Don Triulzi, a perfon very much in years, who had ftudied thefe characters, and had formed fome ingenious conjectures about them.

The reft of this day was fpent in queft of old books, and the evening in hearing mufic. Chiefa and Monza feem, and are faid to be the two beft compofers for the ftage here at prefent. Serbelloni, a *contr'alto caftrato*, who was in England fome

---

* A fpecimen of this notation will be given in the General Hiftory of Mufic.

years

years ago, has had a difpenfation to become a prieft, and now only fings in the
church.

Tuefday 24. This morning a folemn
proceffion paffed through the ftreets to
the church of St. Ambrofe for rain, on
which account the public library was not
open, which was a great difappointment
to me, being the laft day I had to ftay
here; but by this time my letters had procured me the notice and countenance of
his Excellency *Count Ferman*, the *Conte
Pò, il Marchefe Menafoglio*, D. *Francefco
Carcano*, the *Abate Bonelli*, and others;
which operated like *magic* in opening
doors and removing difficulties; and upon
my prefenting myfelf at the Ambrofian
Library with the *Abate Bonelli*, it was inftantly opened; and, indeed, for the firft
time, all its treafures; the moft curious
MSS. were now difplayed; among which
were feveral books of Petrarca's and Leonardo da Vinci's own hand-writing. I

7   was

was likewife fhewn feveral very ancient MSS. upon *papyrus*, well preferved. In fhort, I was made ample amends this morning for former difappointments, being carried into a room containing nothing but MSS. to the amount of fifteen thoufand volumes.

From hence the *Abate* carried me to *Padre Sacchi*, a learned mufician here, as to theory; he has publifhed two very curious books, relative to mufic, which I had before purchafed. He received me very courteoufly, and we entered deeply into converfation on the fubject of them and of my journey. He was fo obliging as to write down my direction, and gave me great encouragement to write to him, if on reading his books I met with any difficulties.

BRESCIA.

Thurfday, July 26. I was only one day in this town, but, it happening to be a holiday, I had the good fortune to hear a boy, at the church of the Jefuits *delle Grazie*,

Grazie, whofe voice and volubility pleafed me much. His name is Carlo Mofchetti, a fcholar of Pietro Pellegrino, *Maeſtra di Capella* of this church, who beat the time during the performance of his motet. This *caſtrato* is not above fourteen or fifteen. He has a compafs of two octaves complete, from the middle C in the fcale to the higheft. His voice is full, when he has time to throw it out; and he executes fwift paſſages with fuch facility, that he is apt to be lavifh and run riot, and now and then is not exactly in tune. But there feems to be good ftuff for a mafter to work upon; his fhake is good, and he promifes to be a great finger. There was a young counter tenor, of whom little is to be faid; a tenor, lefs; and a bafe that drove me out of the church.

At a kind of Magdalen Hofpital in this place, the women were finging and playing moft furioufly; the mufic was in the old ftile, full of fugues upon hackneyed
fubjects

fubjects. Thefe females do the whole
bufinefs, upon fuch occafions, themfelves; play the organ, violins, and bafes:
the performance indeed was fo coarfe,
that I had foon enough of it. I heard
no organs in this town that feemed to be
well toned, but then they are much ornamented, and, like the French opera,
more calculated to pleafe the eye than
the ear. The pipes here are never gilt,
though fometimes the frame and cafe are,
and have not a bad effect.

The theatre at Brefcia is very fplendid,
but it is much lefs than that at Milan,
with refpect to length; the height is the
fame. The proportion of boxes round
each theatre is as one hundred to thirty-
four: there are five rows in each, fo that
this houfe feems much higher than that
at Milan. The boxes are more ornamented with glaffes, paintings, front-
cloths of velvet, or rich filks fringed;
more room is allowed here in the pit, to
each auditor, than at Milan; every feat

I   turns

turns up, and is locked till the person comes who has taken it, and here every row, and every box of each row, is numbered, as in our playhouses, when the pit and boxes are laid together. The comedy was *Il Saggio Amico*, the Prudent Friend, written by Goldoni, it was the first I had ever seen in Italy without a Harlequin, Colombine, Pierro, and Dottore: it was more like a regular comedy than the Italian pieces usually are. There was a *Milordo Inglese* in it, who gave away his zechins by handfuls, with which the audience was very much pleased. Some of the actors came on with candles in their hands; it never struck me before, but, on the English and French stage, where this is not practised, probability suffers when the transactions of the piece are supposed to happen in the night.

Here was a burletta in run, under the direction of Signor Leopoldo Maria Scherli, *Maestro di Capella*; the fingers were Giovanni Simoni, Giuseppe Francefchini,

cefchini, Niccola Menichelli, Angiola Dotti, Geltrude Dotti, Terefa Menichelli, Terefa Monti, but, for my misfortune, they did not perform while I was at Brefcia.

At the fign of the *Gambero* or Lobfter, where I lodged, and in the next room to mine, there was a company of opera fingers, who feemed all very jolly; they were juft come from Ruffia, where they had been fourteen or fifteen years. The principal finger among them, I found, upon enquiry, to be the *Caftrato* Luini Bonetto. He is faid to be ftill very rich, though he loft in one night, at play, ten thoufand pounds of the money he had gained *per la fua virtù*. He is a native of Brefcia; was welcomed home by a band of mufic, at the inn, the night of his arrival, and by another the night before his and my departure, confifting of two violins, a mandoline, French horn, trumpet, and violoncello; and, though in the dark, they played long concertos, with

I 2 folo

folo parts for the mandoline. I was furprifed at the memory of thefe performers;
in fhort, it was excellent *ftreet* mufic,
and fuch as we are not accuftomed to;
but ours is not a climate for ferenades.
The famous Venetian dancer, La Colonna, was likewife juft arrived from Ruffia,
and in the fame houfe; they were all
going to Venice.

VERONA.

There was no opera in this city, ferious or comic, when I arrived in it,
July 28; however, I was conducted to
the famous amphitheatre, faid to have
been built by Auguftus, or, at leaft,
about his time; perhaps by Vitruvius,
who was not only his architect, but a native of Verona. The infide has been
lately repaired, and is entire: it has forty-
fix rows of feats, of rough white marble;
is of an oval figure, the greateft diameter
being two hundred and thirty-three feet;

and

and leaft one hundred and thirty-fix : the
inhabitants fay that it will contain fixty
thoufand perfons, which is more than
twice the number at prefent in Verona.
It was here that the people were formerly
amufed with wild beafts, and upon my
entrance into it, I really thought it had
been ftill appropriated to that purpofe;
for the roaring and noife which affailed
my ears, feemed to proceed from nothing
human; when, behold, upon a nearer
approach I found it was only *Pantalone*
and *Brighello*, who had been baited and
beaten by Harlequin; indeed this gentleman's wit had great force to-night,
and, I believe, contributed more to the
happinefs of the fpectators, than ever the
elephants, lions, or tigers did in former
times. The comedy, in which thefe
characters were introduced, was reprefented in all its buffoon perfection; and
I now faw, for the firft time, *Harlequin,*
Brighello, Pantalone, and *Colombina,* in
true Italian purity. The ftage was erect-

ed

ed in the middle of the *arena*; there were only two boxes, one on each side the stage: the area before the stage made a kind of pit, where the better sort of company sat on chairs The next best places were on the steps, about twelve deep, railed off from the rest of the steps, which may be regarded as the upper gallery; but all this in the open air, and the seats the naked marble. Here is a modern theatre, but that is only used in the winter for the opera *.

VICENZA.

There was neither opera nor comedy at this place when I passed through it, nor should I have mentioned this city in

---

* The short space of time I staid at Verona, was not sufficient for many musical enquiries, but I was afterwards informed by an English gentleman, who had resided several years in that city, that it contains, besides several able professors, a great number of *dilettanti*, who both perform and compose in a superior manner.

my

my journal, had I not been entertained, during dinner, with a kind of vocal mufic which I had not before heard in Italy: it confifted of a pfalm, in three parts, performed by boys of different ages, who were proceeding from their fchool to the cathedral, in proceffion, with their mafter, a prieft, at their head, who fung the bafe. There was more melody than ufual in this kind of mufic; and though they marched through the ftreet very faft, yet they fung very well in time and tune. Thefe boys are a kind of religious *prefs-gang*, who feize all other boys they can find in their way to the church, in order to be catechifed.

In coming from Verona to this city, I. overtook a great number of pilgrims, young men, who were going to Venice to vifit the tomb of St. Francis; they ufed to go to Loretto once a year, but the fenate has forbidden them to go out of the Venetian territories. Several of them marched in large companies, and fung, or rather

I 4   chanted,

chanted, hymns and pſalms in *canto fermo*.

PADUA.

This city has been rendered no leſs famous, of late years, by the reſidence of Tartini, the celebrated compoſer and per-former on the violin, than in ancient times, by having given birth to the great hiſtorian Livy. But Tartini died a few months before my arrival here, an event which I regarded as a particular misfor-tune to myſelf, as well as a loſs to the whole muſical world; for he was a pro-feſſor, whom I was not more deſirous to hear perform, than ambitious to converſe with. I viſited the ſtreet and houſe where he had lived; the church and grave where he was buried; his buſt, his ſucceſſor, his executor, and every thing, however mi-nute and trivial, which could afford me the leaſt intelligence concerning his life and character, with the zeal of a pilgrim at Mecca : and though, ſince his death,

all

all thefe particulars are become hiftorical, and hardly belong to the *prefent ftate*
of mufic; yet I fhould be inclined to
prefent the reader with a fketch of his
life, if my books and papers collected in
the Venetian ftate, among which are the
materials I acquired at Padua concerning
Tartini, were arrived. As it is, I fhall
only fay, that he was born at Pirano, in
Iftria, in 1692; that, in his early youth,
having manifefted an attachment to a
young perfon, who was regarded as un-
worthy of being allied to his family, his
father fhut him up; and during his con-
finement he amufed himfelf with mufical
inftruments, in order to divert his melancholy; fo that it was by mere accident
he difcovered in himfelf the feeds of thofe
talents which afterwards grew into fo
much eminence.

M. de la Lande fays he had from his
own mouth the following fingular anecdote, which fhews to what degree his
imagination was inflamed by the genius

of

of compofition. " He dreamed one
" night, in 1713, that he had made a
" compact with the Devil, who promifed
" to be at his fervice on all occafions;
" and during this vifion every thing
" fucceeded according to his mind, his
" wifhes were prevented, and his defires
" always furpaffed by the affiftance of
" his new fervant. In fhort, he imagined
" he gave the Devil his violin, in order
" to difcover what kind of a mufician he
" was; when, to his great aftonifhment,
" he heard him play a folo fo fingularly
" beautiful, and executed with fuch fu-
" perior tafte and precifion, that it fur-
" paffed all he had ever heard or con-
" ceived in his life. So great was his
" furprife, and fo exquifite his delight
" upon this occafion, that it deprived
" him of the power of breathing. He
" awoke with the violence of this fenfa-
" tion, and inftantly feized his fiddle, in
" hopes of expreffing what he had juft
" heard, but in vain, he, however, then
" com-

" compofed a piece, which is perhaps,
" the beft of all his works, (he called it
" the Devil's Sonata) but it was fo in-
" ferior to what his fleep had produced,
" that he declared he fhould have broken
" his inftrument, and abandoned mufic
" for ever, if he could have fubfifted by
" any other means." *

He married early a wife of the Xan-
tippe fort, and his patience upon the moft
trying occafions was always truly Socra-
tic. He had no other children than his
fcholars, of whom his care was conftantly
paternal. Nardini, his firft, and favourite
pupil, came from Leghorn to fee him in
his ficknefs, and attend him in his laft
moments, with true filial affection and
tendernefs. During the latter part of his
life he played but little, except at the
church of St. Anthony of Padua, to
which he had devoted himfelf fo early as
the year 1722, where, though he had a
falary of four hundred ducats a year, yet
his attendance was only required on great
fefti-

* *Voyage d'un Franç̈ s.* Tom 8

feſtivals; but ſo ſtrong was his zeal for the ſervice of his patron ſaint, that he ſeldom let a week paſs without regaling him to the utmoſt power of his palſied nerves.

He died univerſally regretted by the Patavinians, who had long been amuſed by his talents, and edified by his piety and good works. To his Excellency Count *Torre Taxis* of Venice, his ſcholar and protector, he bequeathed his MS. muſic; and to the profeſſor *Padre Colombo*, who had long been his friend and counſellor, he left the care of a poſthumous work, of which, though chiefly mathematical, the theory of ſound makes a conſiderable part *.

There was a public function performed for him at Padua, March 31, 1770, at which a funeral oration was pronounced by the *Abate Franceſco Fanzago*, and an anthem performed, which was compoſed

---

* In this work he propoſed to remove the obſcurity, and explain the difficulties of which he is accuſed in his former Treatiſes.

on the occafion by Signor **P. Maeftro**
Valloti.

His merit, both as a compofer and
performer, is too well known to need a
panegyric here: I fhall only fay, that as
a compofer, he was one of the few original geniuffes of this age, who conftantly
drew from his own fource; that his melody was full of fire and fancy, and his
harmony, though learned, yet fimple and
pure, and as a performer, that his flow
movements evince his tafte and expreffion, and his lively ones his great hand.
He was the firft who knew and taught
the power of the bow; and his knowledge of the finger-board is proved by a
thoufand beautiful paffages, to which that
alone could give birth. His fcholar,
Nardini, who played to me many of his
beft folos, as I thought, very well, with
refpect to correctnefs and expreffion, affured me that his dear and honoured
mafter, as he conftantly called him, was
as much fuperior to himfelf, in the performance

formance of the fame folos, both in the pathetic and brilliant parts, as he was to any one of his fcholars.

With regard to the complaint made by common readers, of obfcurity in his Treatife of Mufic, and the abufe of mathematics, of which he is accufed by men of fcience, they are points which this is not the place to difcufs. Perhaps a more exact character of this work cannot be given than that of M. Roufleau, who fays, "If the Syftem of the celebrated Tartini is not that of nature, it is at leaft "that of which the principles are the moft "fimple, and from which all the laws "of harmony feem to arife in a lefs ar-"bitrary manner, than in any other "which has been hitherto publifhed *." That his Syftem is full of new and ingenious ideas, which could only arife

* Since this Journal was prepared for the prefs, a book has been publifhed under the title of *Principles and Power of Harmony*, from which I have received the higheft pleafure that an elegant, clear, and mafterly performance can give Who the author

from a fuperior knowledge in his art;
may be difcovered through its veil
of obfcurity; and his friend *Padre Colombo* accounted to me for that obfcurity
and appearance of want of true fcience,
by confeffing that Tartini, with all the
parade of figures, and folutions of prob-
lems, was no mathematician, and that he
did not underftand common arithmetic
well. However, he faw more than he
could exprefs by terms or principles bor-
rowed from any other fcience; and though
neither a geometrician or an algebraift, he
had a facility and method of calculating peculiar to himfelf, by which, as he could fatisfy his own mind, he fuppofed he could
inftruct others. The truth is, that, with
refpect to the myfteries of the fcience,
which he feems to have known intuitively,
he is fometimes intelligible, and fometimes otherwife; but I have fuch an
opinion of Tartini's penetration and faga-

is I know not, but he feems perfectly to underftand
Tartini's principles, and to have done juftice to his
genius, without being partial to his defects.

city

city in his mufical enquiries, that when he is obfcure, I fuppofe it to be occafioned either by his aiming too much at concife-nefs in explaining himfelf, by the infuffi-ciency of common language to exprefs un-common ideas, or that he foars above the reach of my conceptions; and in this cafe I am ready to apply to him what Socrates faid to Euripides, upon being afked by that poet how he liked the writings of Heraclitus—" What I under-" ftand is excellent, which inclines me " to believe that what I do not under-" ftand is excellent likewife."

He is fucceeded in the church of *St. Antonio* by his fcholar, Signor Guglietto Tromba, a young man of merit.

On my arrival at Padua I was extreme-ly defirous of feeing the famous church of Saint Antonio, as well as of hearing the fervice performed in it; and, fup-pofing my Reader to be poffeffed of a fmall portion of my impatience, I fhall haften to give him a fhort defcription of

this

this fabrick; and an account of its mufical eftablifhments

It is a large old Gothic building, and
is called here, by way of excellence, *il
Santo, the* Saint. It has fix domes or
cupolas, of which the two largeft compofe the nave; but though it is only the
fecond church in rank, it is the firft in
fame and veneration at Padua. It is extremely rich, and fo much ornamented,
as to appear crowded with paintings and
fculpture. At the entrance into the
choir the majeftic appearance of four immenfe organs is very ftriking, of which
the front pipes are fo highly polifhed
as to have the appearance of burnifhed
filver: the frames too are richly carved
and gilt. Thefe four organs are all
alike; there are no pannels to the frames,
but the pipes are feen on three fides of a
fquare.

There are on common days forty performers employed in the fervice of this
church; eight violins, four violetti or

K

tenors, four violoncellos, four double bafes, and four wind inftruments, with fixteen voices. There are eight *caftrati* in falary, among whom is Signor Gaetano Guadagni, who, for tafte, expreffion, figure, and action, is at the head of his profeffion. His appointment is four hundred ducats a year, for which he is required to attend only at the four principal feftivals. The firft violin has the fame falary. The fecond *foprano*, Signor Cafati, has a feeble voice, but is reckoned to fing with infinite tafte and expreffion. The famous Antonio Vandini is the principal violoncello, and Matteo Biffioli Brefciano the firft hautbois in this felect band.

Signor Francefco Antonio Valloti, the *Maeftro di Capella*, is a native of Piedmont; Dr. Marfili, the worthy profeffor of botany here, to whofe friendly offices, during my ftay at Padua, I have innumerable obligations, did me the favour to introduce me to this eminent mafter. He is efteemed

one

one of the firſt compoſers for the church
in Italy, and in the frequent converſa-
tions I had with him, I found him to be
a good theoriſt as well as practical muſi-
cian *. He is a churchman, of the order
of St. Francis, near ſeventy years of age;
is in poſſeſſion of ſeveral ſcarce and valuable books on the ſubject of muſic, from
which he permitted me to make extracts: and was ſo obliging as to ſhew
me two large book-caſes filled with the
ſcores of his own compoſitions; ſome for
voices only, and ſome for voices and inſtruments, among which is the funeral
anthem for Tartini; I obtained copies of
ſeveral of theſe. He likewiſe communicated to me part of a treatiſe of his own
writing, in MS. upon modulation; which,
as it is leſs metaphyſical, and has leſs of

---

* Tartini ſpeaks of Padre Vallotı ın the following
manner, " He was formerly a moſt excellent per-
" former on the organ, as he ıs now a moſt excel-
" lent compoſer, and thorough maſter of his art."
Trattato dı Muſica, p 100—*Padova* 1754.

mathematics

mathematics in it than Tartini's Treatise, so it is more clear, and seems more likely to be generally useful, if it should be published.

I was sorry, upon leaving Padua, to quit this good father, who is of so amiable a character, that it is impossible to know and not esteem him. He promised me two of his masses in score, as soon as they could be transcribed *, and pressed me to send him a copy of my book when published, he read my plan with great attention, and over-rated it so far as to say it was a public concern to Italy.

The theatre of Padua is handsome and convenient, it is approached by two magnificent stone stair-cases, and its form is nearly oval. There are in it five rows of boxes, twenty-nine in each, which would perhaps be more pleasing to the eye if they did not project one over the other.

* Since my arrival in England I have received advice of his having sent them to Venice, in order to be forwarded to England

The

The pit contains one hundred and fifty seats, which turn up, and have padlocks fixed to them, the boxes have sliding shutters Between the grand escaliers and the theatre is a room for play, called *Camera di Ridotto*. In June there was a serious opera in it, during the fair of St. Anthony; at that time Padua is very gay, and full of company from Venice and the neighbouring cities. The composer was Signor Sacchini, a Neapolitan, who is Master to the *Conservatorio* of the *Ospidaletto* at Venice. The first woman was Camilla Mattei, sister to Colomba Mattei, who was in England eight or nine years ago; and the two principal men were Signor Potenza, who was in England at the same time as Colomba Mattei, and a famous tenor, *il Cavalier Guglielmi Ettori*, in the service of the Elector of Bavaria, who was more applauded than all the rest. The two principal dancers were M Pic, and Signora Binetti, the subject of the opera, Scipio in Carthage.

K 3   *Thursday,*

Thurfday, Auguft 2. This morning I had the honour, in company with Dr. Marfili, to breakfaft with the Profeffor of Mathematics, *Padre Colombo*, with whom I had a long converfation relative to Tartini and his pofthumous work, mentioned above.

From hence I went to St. Anthony's church, where, it being *the Day of Pardons*, there was a mafs, with folo verfes of *Padre Valloti*'s compofition, who was there to beat the time; but the two principal fingers, Signor Guadagni, and Signor Cafati, being abfent, little remains to be faid of the execution of this mufic, as far as the vocal was concerned, the writing, however, was good, the harmony pure, the modulation mafterly, and the ftile grave and fuitable to the church. But I found that two of the four organs were more than fufficient to over-power the voices; and *Padre Valloti* told me that the noife ufed to be ftill more intolerable, but that he had reduced, by one at a time, the

four

four organs, which were formerly played all at once, to two. The whole four never play now but for the common fervice, when there are no other performers than the priefts. The firft organift at prefent, Signor Domenico Locatello, is reckoned an able artift *; but it were to be wifhed that he and his colleague would accompany the voices and inftruments, which are good, and well worth hearing, with the choir organs only, as we do in England; for, otherwife, nothing *but* the organs can be heard: they are, indeed, fine toned inftruments, but fo powerful, as to render all the reft of the performance ufelefs.

Though it was not a great feftival, yet the band was more numerous than ordinary. I wanted much to hear the celebrated hautbois Matteo Biffioli, and the famous old Antonio Vandini, on the violoncello,

* It is but juftice to fay that I heard him play the organ alone feveral times during the *offertorio*, in a very folemn and mafterly manner.

K 4

who,

who, the Italians fay, plays and expreffes
a parlare, that is, in fuch a manner as to
make his inftrument *fpeak*; but neither
had folo parts However, I give thefe
two performers credit for great abilities,
as they are highly extolled by their countrymen, who muft, by the frequent hearing of excellent performers of all kinds,
infenfibly become good judges of mufical
merit People accuftomed to bad mufic,
may be pleafed with it, but thofe, on the
contrary, who have been long ufed to good
mufic, and performers, *cannot*. It is remarkable that Antonio, and all the other
violoncello players here, hold the bow in
the old-fafhioned way, with the hand
under it. The choir of this church is
immenfe; the bafes are all placed on
one fide, the violins, hautbois, French
horns, and tenors on the other, and the
voices half in one organ-loft, and half in
another, but, on account of their diftance
from each other, the performers were
not always exact in keeping time.

The

The day before my departure from Padua, I visited Signor Tromba, Tartini's scholar and successor. He was so obliging as to play several of his master's solos, particularly two which he had made just before his death, of which I begged a copy, regarding these last drops of his pen as sacred relics of so great and original a genius.

VENICE.

I had many enquiries to make, and had very sanguine expectations from this city, with regard to the music of past times as well as the present. The church of St. Marc has had a constant supply of able masters, from the time of Adriano, Zarlino's predecessor, to Galuppi, its present worthy composer. Venice has likewise been one of the first cities in Europe that has cultivated the musical drama or opera : and, in the graver stile, it has been honoured with a Lotti and a

Mar-

Marcello. Add to thefe advantages the
conſervatorios eſtabliſhed here, and the
ſongs of the *Gondolieri*, or Water-men,
which are ſo celebrated, that every muſical
collector of taſte in Europe is well furniſh-
ed with them, and it will appear that my
expectations were well grounded.

. The firſt muſic I heard here was in the
ſtreet, immediately on my arrival, performed by an itinerant band of two fiddles, a violoncello, and a voice, who,
though as unnoticed here as ſmall-coal-
men or oyſter-women in England, performed ſo well, that in any other country of Europe they would not only have
excited attention, but have acquired ap-
plauſe, which they juſtly merited. Theſe
two violins played difficult paſſages very
neatly, the baſe ſtopped well in tune,
and the voice, which was a woman's,
was well toned, and had ſeveral eſſentials
belonging to that of a good ſinger, ſuch as
compaſs, ſhake, and volubility; but I ſhall
not mention all the performances of this
kind

kind which I met with here; as they happened so frequently, the repetition would be tiresome.

This city is famous for its *conservatorios* or musical schools, of which it has four, the *Ospidale della Pietà*, the *Mendicanti*, the *Incurabile*, and the *Ospidaletto a S. Giovanni e Paulo*, at each of which there is a performance every Saturday and Sunday evening, as well as on great festivals. I went to that of the *Pietà*, the evening after my arrival, Saturday, August 4. The present *Maestro di Capella* is Signor Furlanetti, a priest, and the performers, both vocal and instrumental, are all girls; the organ, violins, flutes, violoncellos, and even French horns, are supplied by these females. It is a kind of Foundling Hospital for natural children, under the protection of several nobles, citizens, and merchants, who, though the revenue is very great, yet contribute annually to its support. These girls are maintained here till they are

married,

married, and all thofe who have talents
for mufic are taught by the beft mafters
of Italy The compofition and performance I heard to-night did not exceed
mediocrity; among the fingers I could
difcover no remarkable fine voice, or
performer poffeffed of great tafte. However, the inftruments finifhed with a fymphony, the firft movement of which, in
point of fpirit, was well wiitten and
executed.

On Sunday morning, Auguft 5, I went
to the Greek church, which has been to-
lerated here ever fince the time of Leo X.
The fervice is performed in the Greek
language, the epiftles and gofpels are
chanted by a high-prieft in a pulpit, and
the prayers and refponfes are fung in a
kind of melody totally different from any
other I had ever heard in or out of the
church. In this there is no organ, but
it is more crowded with ornaments, and
its ceremonials are more numerous than
in any of the Romifh churches

From

From thence I went to St. Marc's, and heard a mass in music, which was sung by the priests, accompanied by the organ only, much in the manner of our full anthems. At St. Luke's church I likewise heard part of a mass with instruments; some of the tenor voices here were good, and the airs written and sung with taste; the music was composed by a priest. There was an excellent fugue in the last chorus, well worked and well performed.

In the afternoon of the same day I went to the hospital *de' Mendicanti*, for orphan girls, who are taught to sing and play, and on Sundays and festivals they sing divine service in chorus. Signor Bertoni is the present *Maestro di Capella*. There was a hymn performed with solos and choiusses, and a *mottetto à voce sola*, which last was very well performed, particularly an accompanied recitative, which was pronounced with great force and energy. Upon the whole, the compositions had some pretty passages, mixed

with

with others that were not very new. The subjects of the fugues and choruffes were trite, and but flightly put together. The girls here I thought accompanied the voices better than at the *Pietà:* as the choruffes are wholly made up of female voices, they are never in more than three parts, often only in two; but thefe, when reinforced by the inftruments, have fuch an effect, that the full complement to the chords is not miffed, and the melody is much more fenfible and marked, by being lefs charged with harmony In thefe hofpitals many of the girls fing in the counter tenor as low as A and G, which enables them always to keep below the *foprano* and *mezzo foprano,* to which they fing the bafe; and this feems to have been long practifed in Italy, as may be feen in the examples of compofition given in the old writers, fuch as Zarlino, Glariano, Kircher, and others, where the loweft part of three is often written in the counter-tenor clef.

From

From hence I went to the *Ofpidaletto*, of which Signor Sacchini is the mafter, and was indeed very much pleafed by the compofition of part of the famous hymn *Salve Regina*, which was finging when I entered the church ; it was new, fpirited, and full of ingenious contrivances for the inftruments, which always *faid* fomething interefting without difturbing the voice. Upon the whole, there feemed to be as much genius in this compofition as in any I had heard fince my arrival in Italy. The performers here too are all orphan girls ; one of them, *la Ferrarefe*, fung very well, and had a very extraordinary compafs of voice, as fhe was able to reach the higheft E of our harpfichords, upon which fhe could dwell a confiderable time, in a fair, natural voice.

Even after this, upon the *Piazza di S. Marco*, I heard a great number of vagrant muficians, fome in bands, accompanying one or two voices, fometimes a fingle voice and guitar, and fonetimes

two

or three guitars together. Indeed it is not to be wondered at, that the street-mufic here is generally neglected; as people are almoft ftunned with it at every corner; but, however, in juftice to the tafte and difcernment of the Italians, it muft be allowed, that when they do admire, it is fomething excellent; and then, they never " damn with faint praife," but exprefs rapture in a manner peculiar to themfelves; they feem to agonize with pleafure too great for the aching fenfe.

They had here, laft Carnival, feven opera-houfes open at once, three ferious, and four comic, befides four play-houfes, and thefe were all crowded every night.

Monday 6. This morning the Doge went in proceffion to the church of S. *Giovanni e Paolo.* I was not only curious to fee this proceffion, but to hear the mufic, which I expected would be very confiderable, and by a great band, however there was only a mafs fung in four

6   parts,

parts, without other inftrument than the organ, but then it was fo good of the kind, fo well executed and accompanied, that I do not remember to have received more pleafure from fuch mufic. One of the organifts of St. Mark's church, who is in orders, attended, and difcovered himfelf, in his voluntaries and interludes, to be a very mafterly performer. The voices were well chofen, and well afforted, no one ftronger than the other; the compofition was of Signor Lotti, and was truly grave and majeftic, confifting of fugues and imitations in the ftile of our beft old church fervices, which have been fo well felected, and publifhed in fo magnificent a manner by Dr Boyce; all was clear and diftinct, no confufion or unneceffary notes; it was even capable of expreffion, particularly one of the movements, into which the performers entered fo well, that it affected me even to tears. The organift here very judicioufly fuffered the voices to be heard in all their purity, in-

L   fomuch

fomuch that I frequently forgot that they were accompanied; upon the whole this feems to be the true ftile for the church: it calls to memory nothing vulgar, light, or prophane; it difpofes the mind to phil-anthrophy, and divefts it of its grofs and fenfual paffions. Indeed my being moved was the mere effect of well-modulated and well-meafured founds, for I knew not the words, which were wholly loft by the diftance; nor is this fpecies of mufic at all favourable to poetry: in the anfwers that are made to the points, the feveral parts all fing different words, fo that no great effects can be produced by them; but notwithftanding this defect, fuch mufic as this, in the fervice of the church, muft ever be allowed to have its merit, however it may be exploded, or unfit for theatrical purpofes.

In confequence of a meffage from Mr. Richie, *Chargé des Affaires* to his Britan-nic Majefty, to whom Sir James Wright had honoured me with a letter, and who

very

very politely and kindly was pleafed to intereft himfelf effectually in my fervice, I was this afternoon favoured with a vifit from Signor Latilla, an eminent compofer here, and had a long converfation with him relative to the fubject of my journey. I found him to be a plain, fenfible man, of about fixty years of age, who had both read and thought much concerning the mufic of the ancients, as well as that of the moderns, to which he has contributed a confiderable fhare for many years paft *. I admired his candour in advifing me to go to the *Incurabili*, to hear the girls perform there, with whom he faid I fhould be much pleafed. They are fcholars of Signor Galuppi, who is *Maeftro di Capella* of this Confervatorio. Unluckily when I arrived there, the performance was begun, however, I had only loft the

* Moft of the comic operas performed in London with fuch fuccefs; in the time of Pertici and Lafchi, were of Latilla's compofition; particularly *La Comedia in Comedia*, *Don Calafcione*, and others. He is uncle to Signor Piccini.

over-

overture, and part of the firſt air. The words were taken from three or four of the Pſalms in Latin, from the hymn *Salve Regina,* and one of the Canticles put into Latin verſe, and in dialogue. I knew not whether I was moſt delighted with the compoſition, or with the execution; both were admirable. Signor Buranello has preſerved all his fire and imagination from the chill blaſts of Ruſſia, whence he is lately returned *. This ingenious, entertaining, and elegant compoſer abounds in novelty, in ſpirit, and in delicacy, and his ſcholars did his muſic great juſtice. Several of them had uncommon talents for ſinging, particularly the *Rota, Paſqua Roſſi,* and the *Ortolani;* the two laſt ſung the Canticle in dialogue. The overture, and the whole of this laſt performance were for two orcheſtras. In the overture, which was full of pretty

* Signor Galuppi is beſt known in Italy by the name of *Buranello,* which he acquired from having been born in the little iſland of Burano, near Venice. He is replaced at Peterſburg by Signor Traetta.

paſ-

paſſages, the two-bands echoed each other. There were two organs, and two pair of French horns. In ſhort, I was extremely entertained by this performance, and the whole company, which was very numerous, ſeemed equally pleaſed. The young ſingers, juſt mentioned, are abſolute nightingales; they have a facility of executing difficult diviſions equal to that of birds. They did ſuch things in that way, eſpecially the *Rota*, as I do not remember to have heard attempted before. The able maſter was diſcoverable in all the cadences of theſe young ſubjects. The inſtrumental parts were very well executed, and the whole indicated a ſuperior genius in the compoſer and conductor of the performance. This muſic, which was of the higher ſort of theatric ſtile, though it was performed in a church, was not mixed with the church ſervice, and the audience ſat the whole time as at a concert; and, indeed, this

might

might be called a *concerto fpirituale* with
great propriety.

Tuefday 7. This morning there was a
mafs in mufic at the church of S *Gaetano*.
It being a great feftival, all the treafures
and relics were expofed to public view,
and there was a very great crowd. The
compofer of the mufic, and the perfon
who beat the time was Signor Menagatto,
a prieft; I cannot fay that I received
much pleafure from this performance,
the organ was coarfe, and poorly played;
the voices only two indifferent tenors, and
a bafe, and the compofition very common, and unmarked by any ftamp of original genius.

The people here, at this feafon, feem
to begin to live only at midnight Then
the canals are crowded with gondolas,
and St Mark's fquare with company;
the banks too of the canals are all peo-
pled, and harmony prevails in every part.
If two of the common people walk together arm in arm, they feem to converfe

in song; if there is company on the water, in a gondola, it is the same; a mere melody, unaccompanied with a second part, is not to be heard in this city: all the ballads in the streets are sung in duo. Luckily for me, this night, a barge, in which there was an excellent band of music, consisting of violins, flutes, horns, bases, and a kettle-drum, with a pretty good tenor voice, was on the great canal, and stopped very near the house where I lodged; it was a piece of gallantry, at the expence of an *inamorato* in order to senerade his mistress. Shakespeare says of nocturnal music,

" Methinks it sounds much sweeter than by day.
" Silence bestows the virtue on it—I think
" The nightingale, if she should sing by day,
" When every goose is cackling, would be thought
" No better a musician than the wren."

Whether the time, place, and manner of performing this music, gave it adventitious and collateral charms, I will not pretend to say; all I know is, that the

symphofymphonies *feemed* to me to be admirable, full of fancy, full of fire; the paffages well contrafted; fometimes the graceful, fometimes the pathetic prevailed; and fometimes, however ftrange it may be thought, even noife and fury had their effect. No one will I believe, at prefent, deny the neceffity of *difcord* in the compofition of mufic in parts; it feems to be as much the effence of mufic, as fhade is of painting; not only as it improves and meliorates concord by oppofition and comparifon, but, ftill further, as it becomes a neceffary ftimulus to the attention, which would languifh over a fucceffion of pure concords. It occafions a momentary diftrefs to the ear, which remains unfatisfied, and even uneafy, till it hears fomething better; for no mufical phrafe *can end* upon a difcord, the ear muft be fatisfied at laft. Now, as difcord is allowable, and even neceffarily oppofed to concord, why may not *noife*, or a feeming jargon, be oppofed to fixed founds

and

and harmonical proportion? Some of the difcords in modern mufic, unknown 'till this century, are what the ear can but juft bear, but have a very good effect as to contraft. The fevere laws of preparing and refolving difcord, may be too much adhered to for great effects; I am convinced, that provided the ear be at length made amends, there are few diffonances too ftrong for it. If, for inftance, the five founds c. d. e. f. g, are all ftruck at the fame inftant on the harpfichord, provided the d and the f are taken foon off, and the three others remain, the ear will not fuffer much by the firft fhock. Or, ftill further; if, inftead of the five founds above-mentioned, the following are ftruck; c d ♮. e. f ✕. g and the d and f# are not held on fo long as the reft, all will end to the fatisfaction of the offended ear.

Wednefday 8. This day was remarkable for no enquiry relative to the prefent ftate of mufic in Italy, however it

deferves

deferves-mention here, on account of the opportunity it afforded me of converfing with the *Abate Martini,* one of the beft judges of every part of mufic, ancient and modern, that I had yet met with. He is an able mathematician, a compofer, and performer. He had travelled into Greece, in order to make obfervations in geography, agriculture, and natural hiftory, but being unable to fatisfy himfelf as he expected, his pride was fo hurt by the difappointment, that he would not publifh any of his remarks or difcoveries. Among other curious enquires, he made many concerning the mufic of the modern Greeks, in hopes it would throw fome light upon that of the ancient. He knows, I believe, as much as any one elfe, about the fyftems of Pythagoras, Ptolemy, and the writers collected by Meibomius, as well as of Rameau and Tartini. He is a great admirer of the works of Marcello, and fings by heart all his cantatas and beft melodies. After

reading

reading my plan, which we difcuffed article by article, he entered much into my views; fhewed me his Grecian and other manufcript papers, and I had great reafon to be fatisfied both with my reception, and the information with which he favoured me.

9*th*. I had this afternoon another long converfation with the fame learned gentleman, who was fo obliging as to bring his manufcript papers concerning Greek mufic, and to defire my acceptance of them. I could not help regarding this prefent as a valuable acquifition, for though the materials it contained were too few for his original purpofe of forming a book, they appeared likely to be of importance in the courfe of a work, in which it is propofed to treat not only of ancient mufic, but of the national mufic of moft parts of the world, from whence fpecimens, or accounts well authenticated can be had. The *Abate* has, however, collected a fet of apophthegms or

pro-

proverbs, which he intends to publiſh, and which will diſcover the manners and miſery of the modern Greeks, per-haps more effectually than any other work could do.

There was muſic this evening at the church of St. Laurence, compoſed and directed by Signor Sacchini, at which, as it was the vigil of this ſaint, there was a great crowd. I ſuffered, as well as every one elſe, too much by the heat, perhaps, to be eaſily pleaſed, and the compoſition ſeemed rather more common than that I had heard of this ingenious maſter before; however, the vocal parts were not ſo well performed, as there were no other ſingers than thoſe of St. Mark's church, who moſt excel in mere church muſic, accompanied only by the organ. The voices were not good enough for long ſolo parts, nor ſtrong enough to get through a large band; however there were many very pleaſing and agreeable movements, and ſome of the choruſſes

were

were well worked in the fugue and oratorio way. But for this kind of mufic, that of Handel will, I believe, ever ftand fuperior to all other writers; at leaft I have heard nothing yet on the continent of equal force and effect. There is often in the compofitions of others, more melody in the folo parts, more delicacy, and more light and fhade, but as to harmony, and contrivance, no one comes near him by many degrees. I muft confefs that I had heard fome of Handel's mufic fo long, and often fo ill performed, that I was fomewhat tired and difgufted with it; but my Italian journey, inftead of lowering the efteem I ever had for the beft writings of that truly great artift, exalted them in my opinion, and, at my return renewed my pleafure in hearing them performed. As yet I had heard little but church mufic in Italy; however, in that ftile, *with inftruments*, all other compofitions appeared feeble by comparifon. The fubjects of the fugues were, in general,

ral,

ral, trivial and common, and the manner of working them dry and artless. Indeed the church stile, *without instruments*, except the organ, was well known in Italy, and all over Europe, long before Handel's time; and melody is certainly much refined since: it is more graceful, more pathetic, and even more gay; but for counter-point, fugues, and choruses of many voices, *with instruments*, I repeat it, I neither have heard, nor do I ever expect to hear him equalled.

10*th*. This morning I went again to the church of the convent of St. Laurence, where, besides a mass of Signor Sacchini's composition, I heard Signor Nazzari, the first violin of Venice, play a concerto; but we have long heard that instrument so well performed upon in England, that nothing is left to admire. However, Signor Nazzari is certainly a very neat and pleasing player; his tone is even, sweet, and full; he plays with great facility and expression, and is, upon the whole,

whole, the beft folo player I had heard on this fide the Alps.

Argus is faid to have had an hundred eyes, and Fame has been painted by the poets *all tongues*; in this place one wifhes to be all *ears* for mufic, and all *eyes* for painting and architecture. To-day there were fo many temptations to a lover of harmony, that it was difficult for him to chufe; for, befides the four confervatorios, there were feveral *accademias* or private concerts. I was invited to one, which affembles on all feftivals, in order to fing the works of Marcello, without other accompaniment than a harpfichord; and as this was different from any other I had been at in Italy, I accepted the invitation; though I wifhed very much to be at the *Incurabili*, where I was fure of entertainment from Buranello and his fcholars.

Several of Marcello's Pfalms were here very well fung by the *Abate Martini* and fome other *dilettanti*, among whom one

had

had a very good bafe voice, and, between
the Pfalms, fung Marcello's famous can-
tata called *Caffandra,* where this compofer has entirely facrificed the mufic to
the poetry, by changing the time or ftile
of his movement at every new idea which
occurs in the words; this may, perhaps,
fhew a compofer to be a very fenfible
man, but at the fame time it muft difcover him to be of a very phlegmatic
turn, and wholly free from the enthufiafm of a creative mufical genius. And,
indeed, fince melody has been allied
to grace and fancy, mufical disjointed
thoughts on various fubjects, would
be but ill received by the public. One
of thefe gentlemen performers was old
enough to remember very well the celebrated Benedetto Marcello, who has
been dead forty-four years, and gave me
feveral anecdotes about him; his family,
which is noble, ftill fubfifts, and the head
of it is now ambaffador from the Venetian ftate at the Porte.

11*th.*

11*th*. This afternoon I went again to the *Pietà*, there was not much company, and the girls played a thousand tricks in singing, particularly in the duets, where there was a trial of skill and of natural powers, as who could go higheſt, loweſt, ſwell a note the longeſt, or run divisions with the greateſt rapidity. They always finiſh with a ſymphony, and laſt Wedneſday they played one by Sarte, which I had before heard in England, at the opera of the *Olimpiade*. The band here is certainly very powerful, as there are in the hoſpital above a thouſand girls, and out of theſe there are ſeventy muſicians, vocal and inſtrumental; at each of the other three hoſpitals there are not above forty, as I was informed by Signor L'Atilla, which are choſen out of about a hundred orphans, as the orignal eſtabliſhment requires. But it has been known that a child, with a fine voice, has been taken into theſe hoſpitals before it was bereaved of father or mother. Children are

M   ſome-

fometimes brought hither to be educated from the towns belonging to the Venetian ftate, upon the Continent, from Padua, Verona, Brefcia, and even from other places, ftill more diftant, for Francefca Gabrieli came from Ferrara, and is therefore called the Ferrarefe. The Confervatorio of the *Pietà* has heretofore been the moft celebrated for its band, and the *Mendicanti* for voices, but in the voices time and accident may occafion great alterations, the mafter may give a celebrity to a fchool of this kind, both by his compofitions and abilities in teaching, and as to voices, nature may fometimes be more kind to the fubjects of one hofpital than another; but as the number is greater at the *Pietà* than at the reft, and confequently the chances of fuperior qualifications more, it is natural to fuppofe that this hofpital will in general have the beft band and the beft voices. At prefent, the great abilities of Signor Galuppi are confpicuous in the performances

ances at the *Incurabili*, which is, in point of mufic, finging, and orcheftra, in my opinion, fuperior to the reft. Next to that, the *Ofpidaletto* takes place of the other two, fo that the *Pietà* feems to enjoy the reputation of being the beft fchool, not for what it *does now*, but for what it *has done*, heretofore.

Sunday 12. This morning, after hearing high mafs well performed at St. Mark's, I went to the patriarchal church of St Peter, and heard it again there, accompanied by a very fine organ, well played on by one of the priefts; after that I went to the Francifcans' church, where one of the Friars likewife was organift, but he played in a very fuperior manner, both as to tafte and harmony: though I vifited thefe churches for the fake of mufic, it was impoffible to keep my eyes off the pictures and architecture But it was here I began to find that thefe two objects of fight were not fo remote from my chief purpofe of writing a hif-

M 2

tory

tory of the pleafures of the ear, as I at
firft imagined, for I frequently, in the
old mafters, met with reprefentations of
mufical inftruments, either of their
own times, or at leaft fuch as they
imagined to be in ufe at the time when
the action of the piece happened; thus
I obferved in a famous picture of the
Marriage of Cana by P Veronefe, in the
Sacrifty of S. Georgio Maggiore, a concert, with a variety of inftruments, of all
which I have made a memorandum : and
I faw this morning, at the Francifcans, a
little picture under the pulpit, by San
Croce, which is much admired; and
thought to be a good deal in the ftile of
Raphael, in which is a concert of che-
rubs and feraphs ; and I obferved among
feveral different kinds of lutes and guitars, an inftrument played with a bow,
refting, like a violin, upon the fhoulder
of the performer, but it had fix ftrings.

After I had feen thefe, and fome more
churches, I had the honour of a long

converſation with *il Conte Torre Taxis*, who is here a perſon of great weight *; he is Superintendant-general of the German and Venetian poſt-office, was a great friend of Tartini, is now in poſſeſſion of all his MS. compoſitionś, ſhewed me a great number of them, and has defended his friend in a pamphlet, of which he did me the honour to give me a copy, againſt ſome remarks made upon his *Trattato di Muſica*, by M. Rouſſeau, in his *Dict. de Muſique.* This nobleman, though young, ſeems to poſſeſs great muſical erudition; to have profited from the converſe and correſpondence of Tartini, and to be an enthuſiaſt for the arts in general. I had great pleaſure in his converſation, in which I communicated to him my plan of a Hiſtory of Muſic, and was pleaſed and enlightened by his obſervations.

* He is of the ſame family with that German prince, better known in France and England by the name of *Tour Taxis*.

In

In the afternoon I ftopped a little while
at the new church of the *Jcfuati*, where
I heard the organ played with a very uncommon brilliancy of execution, by one
of the Dominicans It was indeed a
ftile of playing more fuitable to the harpfichord than organ, but, in its way, was
very mafterly and powerful.   There are
fome reed ftops in this inftrument which
I had never heard before, and with which
the performer produced effects that I was
unable to account for.   I had not time to
make enquiries, as I took this church
only in my way to the *Incurabili*, where
I was fo pleafed, both with the compofition and performance, that in fpeaking
of them I fhall find it difficult to avoid
hyperboles.

- It feems as if the genius of Signor
Galuppi, like that of Titian, became
more animated by age. He cannot now
be lefs than feventy years old, and yet it is
generally allowed here that his laft **operas,**
and his laft compofitions for the church,
abound

abound with more fpirit, tafte, and fancy,
than thofe of any other period of his life.
This evening the Latin Pfalms that were
fung by the orphan girls, gave me great
reafon to concur in the common opinion,
for out of ten or twelve movements,
there was not one that could be pronounced *indifferent*. There were feveral admirable, accompanied recitatives, and the
whole abounded with new paffages, with
good tafte, good harmony, and good fenfe.
His accompaniments, in particular, are always ingenious, but, though full, free
from that kind of confufion which dif-
turbs and covers the voice. I muft likewife do juftice to the orcheftra, which is
here under the moft exact difcipline; no
one of the inftrumental performers feemed
ambitious of fhining at the expence of
the vocal part, but all were under that
kind of fubordination which is requifite
in a *fervant* to a *fuperior*. Of thefe
young fingers I have fpoken rather warm-
ly before, but in this performance they

dif-

difcovered ftill new talents and new cultivation. Their mufic of to-night was rather more grave than that which I had heard here before, and I thought they were more firm in it, that their intonations were more exact, and, as more time was allowed for it, a greater volume of voice by the two principal fubjects was thrown out But in their clofes, I know not which aftonifhed me moft, the compafs of voice, variety of paffages, or rapidity of execution; indeed all were fuch as would have merited and received great applaufe in the firft operas of Europe. I dwell the longer on thefe performances, as, at prefent, the theatres of Venice are all fhut; but the only difference between this kind of church mufic, and that of the drama, confifts in the choruffes, thofe of the church are long, elaborate, and fometimes well written. Thofe who fuppofe all the church mufic of Italy to be as light and airy as that of the opera, are miftaken, it is only on feftivals that

modern

modern mufic can be heard in any of the churches. The mufic of the cathedrals, on common days, is in a ftile as grave and as ancient as that of our church fervices of two hundred years ftanding; and in the parifh chuiches it is a mere *canto fermo*, or chant, fung in unifon by the priefts only; fometimes with the organ, but more frequently without. If we compare the mufic of Mr. Handel's firft oratorios with the operas he compofed about the fame time, it will appear that the airs of the one are often as gay as thofe of the other. And as to the choruffes of an opera, which are all to be in action, and performed by memory, they muft of courfe be fhorter and lefs laboured than thofe of an oratorio, where every finger has his part before him, and where a compofer is allowed fufficient time to difplay his abilities in every fpecies of what is called by muficians good writing.

From

From the *Incurabili* I had the honour to be carried by his Excellency Signor Murin Giorgi, to an *accademia*, at the *Casa Grimani*, where I first had the pleasure to hear Signora Baffa, a noble Venetian lady. She has long been reckoned the best performer on the harpsichord of all the ladies of Venice, and I found that she played very neatly, and with much taste and judgment. The company consisted of the chief nobility of Venice, the three persons I have named being among the first class. They did great justice in this assembly to the abilities of Mrs Cassandra Wynn, from England, who was there last year, and had left behind her the character of a very great player.

Tuesday 14. This evening being the vigil of the Assumption, there were musical performances at three different churches. I went first to that of the *Celestia*, the vespers were composed and directed by the *Maestro* of the Pietà, Signor

Signor Furlanetto, there were two orcheſtras, both well filled with vocal and
inſtrumental performers : the overture
was ſpirited, and the firſt chorus good,
in *Contra Punto*; then there was a long
ſymphony in dialogue, between the two
orcheſtras, and an air well accompanied,
though but indifferently ſung. After
this an air in dialogue with the chorus,
which had a good effect : an air for a
tenor voice, of little merit, and one for a
baſe, which was ingeniouſly put together,
making uſe by turns of all the principal inſtruments : I did not ſtay out the whole performance, but what I heard ſeemed ſuperior
to any compoſition that I had before met
with of this author, he availed himſelf
of the two orcheſtras, and produced ſeveral effects which, with one, would have
been impracticable.

From hence I went to the *Oſpidaletto*,
where the muſic and muſicians ſpoke a
different language. The performance was
a Latin oratorio; *Machabæorum Mater*;
the

the mufic was by Signor Sacchini, there
were fix characters in it, the principal was
performed by Francefca Gabrieli: it was
divided into two parts; the firft was
over before I arrived, for which I was
very forry, as what remained delighted
me extremely, both as to the compofition, which was excellent, and the finging which had infinite merit. When
I entered the church the *Ferrarefe* was
fpeaking an admirable accompanied recitative in fuch a manner as is feldom
heard; it was terminated by a *Bravura*
air, with a pathetic fecond part in Jomelli's oratorio ftyle, but by no means
in his paffages; there was then a recitative and flow air by Laura Conti, who is
poffeffed of no great power of voice; it
is a mere *voce di Camera*; but fhe has infinite expreffion and tafte, and charmed
me in a different way: then followed another recitative, and after it a duet, which
was truly fublime; it was extremely
well executed by Domenica Pafquati and

Ippolita

Ippolita Santi; upon the whole, Signor Sacchini rifes in my opinion, and according to my feelings and intelligence he is the fecond in Venice, having no fuperior there but Signor Galuppi. The finging I heard at this hofpital to-night would, as well as that of the *Mendicanti*, I am certain, receive great applaufe in the firft opera of Europe.

Wednefday 15. I went this morning to St. Mark's church, at which, being a feftival, the doge was prefent. I there heard high mafs performed under the direction of Signor Galuppi, compofer of the mufic. Upon this occafion there were fix orcheftras, two great ones in the galleries of the two principal organs, and four lefs, two on a fide, in which there were likewife fmall organs. I was placed very advantageoufly in one of the great organ lofts, with Signor L'Atilla, affiftant to Signor Galuppi *. The mu-

* This inftrument has pedals, and but one row of box keys.

fic,

fic, which was in general full and grave, had a great effect, though this church is not very happily formed for mufic, as it has five domes or cupolas, by which the found is too much broken and reverberated before it reaches the ear

From hence I went again to the *Celestià*, which church was very much crowded. The mafs was fet to mufic by Signor Furlanetto, mafter to the *Pietà:* the refources of this compofer are very few; he has little fire and lefs variety, but he fins more on the fide of genius than learning, as his harmony is good, and modulation regular and warrantable; but I muft own, that his mufic is to me tirefome, and leaves behind it a languor and diffatiffaction; whereas that of Signor Galuppi and Sacchini always exhilerates and enlivens Signor Nazari played here a concerto on the violin in a very neat and pleafing manner. I know not of whofe compofition, but it was by no means remarkable for novelty After dinner I

went

went to the church of Santa Maria Maggiore to fee fome pictures, and ftumbled
on mufic, but fuch mufic as I did not
think it poffible for the people of Italy to
bear. The organ was out of tune, other
inftruments out of time, and the voices
were both; then the compofition feemed
juft fuch ftuff as a boy who was learning
counter-point would produce after the
firft two or three leffons. After I had
feen the two beft pictures in the
church, the famous St. John the Baptift,
by Titian, and Noah's ark by Giacomo
Baffano, I ran away from this mufic to
the *Incurabili*, where Buranello's nightingales, the Rota, and Pafqua Roffi, poured
balm into my wounded ears. There was
not much company, and the girls did not
exert themfelves; however, after what I
had juft heard, their performance was
ravifhing; and it was not without regret
that I reflected upon this being the *laft
time* I fhould hear it.

Thurfday

Thurſday 16. My viſit to Signor Galuppi this morning was long, profitable,
and entertaining. I was very glad to
find upon ſeeing him, that time had
ſpared the perſon as well as genius of
this excellent compoſer. He is ſtill lively and alert, and likely to delight the
lovers of muſic many years. His character and converſation are natural, intelligent, and agreeable. He is in figure
little and thin, but has very much the
look of a gentleman. Signor Galuppi
was a ſcholar of the famous Lotti, and
very early taken notice of as a good harpſichord player, and a genius in compoſition. He was ſo obliging as to preſent
me to Signora Galuppi; to ſhew me his
houſe; an admirable picture of a ſleeping
child, by P. Veroneſe, which has been
long in his wife's family; and to carry
me into his working-room, with only a
little clavichord in it, where, he told me,
he *dirtied paper*. His family has been
very large, but all his children, except
three

three or four, are now well married. He
has the appearance of a regular family
man, and is efteemed at Venice as much
for his private character as for his public
talents. He feems, however, rather hurt
at the encouragement and protection
which fome ecclefiaftical dunces, among
whom is F——, meet with as compofers
here Indeed, except Sacchini, his fecond, he ftands fo high among the prefent
race of muficians in Venice, that he feems
a giant among dwarfs: he was fo obliging,
at my requeft, as to promife me a piece
of his compofition, which has not yet
been made public, as a relick and mark
of his friendfhip. I fhewed him my
plan, and we talked over that, and mufic
and muficians, very cordially, and with
fimilar fentiments. his definition of good
mufic I think admirable, and though
fhort, very comprehenfive. It confifts,
he fays, of *vaghezza, chiarezza, e buona modulazione**. He and Signor L'A-

* Beauty, clearnefs, and good modulation.

tilla,

tilla, among many other particulars, re-
collected the names of all the great masters
of the conservatorios, and had patience to
let me write them down These gentlemen likewise informed me that the expence of the conservatorios, on account
of music, is very inconsiderable, there
being but five or six masters to each for
singing and the several instruments, as
the elder girls teach the younger. The
Maestro di Capella seldom does more than
compose and direct: sometimes, indeed,
he writes down *closes*, and usually attends
the last rehearsal and first public performance.

A succession of able masters has constantly been employed in these schools:
Hasse was once *Maestro* to the *Incurabili*,
and has left a *Miserere*, which is still performed there in Passion Week, and is,
according to the Abate Martini, a wonderful composition *.

* I obtained, before I left Venice, a copy of
it, and since my arrival in England, I have been
honoured

Signor Galuppi feemed to have full employment here, even in fummer, when there are no operas, as he is firft *Maeftro di Capella* of St. Mark, and of the *Incurabili*. He has a hundred zechins a year as domeftic organift to the family of Giitti, and is organift of another church, of which I have forgot the name. He certainly merits all that can be done for him, being one of the few remaining original geniuffes of the beft fchool perhaps that Italy ever faw. His compofitions are always ingenious and natural, and I may add, that he is a good contrapuntift, and a friend to poetry. The fiift appears by his fcores, and the latter by the melodies he fets to words, in which the expreffion of his mufic always correfponds with the fenfe of the author, and often improves it. His compofitions for the church are but little

honoured with a letter from Count Bujovich, of Venice, with feveral interefting particulars relative to the rife and progrefs of thefe mufical inftitutions.

known

known in England; to me they appear excellent *, for though many of the
airs are in the opera ftile, yet, upon occafion, he fhews himfelf to be a very
able writer in the true church ftile, which
is grave, with good harmony, good modulation, and fugues well worked.

I was this evening at a fecond *Accademia*, at Signor Grimani's, which was
much more confiderable than the firft.
Signor Sacchini was there, and feveral
of the principal muficians of Venice. La
Signora Regina Zocchi, a lady who had
her mufical education at the *Incurabili*,
under the celebrated Signor Haffe, and
who is now well married, and received, and even courted by the firft
people here, fung: fhe has a very powerful voice, and good fhake, with great volubility and expreffion. D Flaminio Tomj,
who has a mere *Voce di Camera*, fung

* I procured at Venice, fome of his motets,
and Giafeppe, an excellent copieft there, undertook
to tranfcribe, and fend after me, two or three of
his maffes.

with

with exquifite tafte. La Signora Baffa performed on the harpfichord, two or three concertos with much grace and precifion. Add to this, that the whole was well heard by a very large company, compofed of the firft nobility of Venice, among whom was Signor Mocenigo, fon to the prefent doge.

Friday 17. I had this morning the honour of a fecond interview with Count Torre Taxis, during which, I had the pleafure to hear his excellency perform on the harpfichord, of which inftrument he is an able mafter; he played voluntaries for a confiderable time, in which he difcovered much fkill in modulation, and I found him worthy of a place on the upper form of the *Tartini* fchool. He fhewed me a great number of maffes, motets, and oratorios of his compofition, for though young, he is already a very voluminous writer. He is poffeffed of a very curious keyed inftrument which was made at Berlin, under

N 3 the

the direction of his Pruffian Majefty : it is, in fhape, like a large clavichord, has feveral changes of ftops, and is occafionally a harp, a harpfichord, a lute, or piano forte ; but the moft curious property of this inftrument is, that by drawing out the keys the hammers are transferred to different ftrings, by which means a compofition may be tranfpofed half a note, a whole note, or a flat third lower at pleafure, without the embarraffment of different notes or clefs, real or imaginary.

Among the *Dilettanti* here, befides Count Taxis, there is a noble Venetian, Signor Giovan Cornaro, remarkable for his genius and fkill in compofition : he had compofed a mafs for a great feftival at a church in Padua, which was performed there, while I was at Venice, with an immenfe band of voices and inftruments.

This evening, in order to make myfelf more fully acquainted with the nature

ture of the confervatorios, and to finifh my mufical enquiries here, I obtained permiffion to be admitted into the mufic fchool of the *Mendicanti*, and was favoured with a concert, which was performed wholly on my account, and lafted two hours, by the beft vocal and inftrumental performers of this hofpital: it was really curious to *fee*, as well as to *hear* every part of this excellent concert, performed by females, violins, tenors, bafes, harpfichord, French horns, and even double bafes; and there was a priorefs, a perfon in years, who prefided: the firft violin was very well played by Antonia Cubli, of Greek extraction; the harpfichord fometimes by Francefca Roffi, *maeftra del coro*, and fometimes by others; thefe young perfons frequently change inftruments. The finging was really excellent in different ftiles; Laura Rifegari and Giacoma Frari, had very powerful voices, capable of filling a large theatre; thefe fung *bravura* fongs, and capital

N 4   fcenes

fcenes felected from Italian operas; and Francefca Tomj, fifter to the Abate of that name, and Antonia Lucuvich, whofe voices were more delicate, confined themfelves chiefly to pathetic fongs, of tafte and expreffion. The whole was very judicioufly mixed, no two airs of a fort followed each other, and there feemed to be great decorum and good difcipline obferved in every particular; for thefe admirable performers, who are of different ages, all behaved with great propriety, and feemed to be well edu-cated. It was here that the two cele-brated female performers, the Archiapate, now Signora Guglielmi, and Signora Maddalena Lombardini Sirmen, who have received fuch great and juft applaufe in England, had their mufical inftructions If I could have ftaid a few days longer at Venice, I might have enjoyed the fame kind of entertainment at the other three confervatorios, having been tempted to continue there by fuch an offer from a
friend

friend who had intereſt ſufficient to procure me a ſight of the *interior diſcipline* of theſe admirable muſical ſeminaries; and I declined this obliging offer with the greater reluctance, as there is not in all Italy, any eſtabliſhment of the ſame kind, but being willing to divide the time I had allowed myſelf for the enquiries I had to make there as equally as poſſible, I reſiſted that temptation as well as ſeveral other offers with which I was honoured, from ſome of the principal nobility, of being admitted to their private concerts; and thus far for the honour of Italy, as well as for my own, I muſt ſay, that I met with the politeſt treatment, and greateſt encouragement and aſſiſtance imaginable, wherever I ſtopt. At Venice my expectations were greatly ſurpaſſed, as I had always been told that the inhabitants, particularly the better ſort, were reſerved and difficult of acceſs.

I

I was indebted for much of my entertainment and information at Venice, to
the affiduity and friendfhip of Mr. Ed-
wards, a young gentleman who was born
in England, but has lived fo long in this
city, that he has wholly loft his verna-
nacular tongue. With this gentleman,
and D. Flaminio Tomj, I went from the
Confervatorio of the *Mendicanti*, to Signor
Grimani's : here the Abate Tomj fung
two or three pathetic airs with more tafte
than I can remember to have heard fince
the death of Palma. There was a great
deal of company, and the mufical performances of various kinds continued till
two or three o'clock in the morning ; at
which time I took a melancholy leave of
Signor Grimani, who had honoured me
with fomething more than mere politenefs and hofpitality ; in a lefs elevated
character I fhould venture to call it friendfhip, but here it could only be conde-
fcending goodnefs.

To

To finifh my account of the mufic of this charming city, I muft obferve, that though the compofers of the Venetian fchool are in general good contrapuntifts, yet their chief charaƈteriftics are delicacy of tafte, and fertility of invention, but many circumftances concur to render the mufic of Venice better, and more general than elfewhere. The Venetians have few amufements but what the theatres afford; walking, riding, and all field-fports, are denied them. This in fome degree accounts for mufic being fo much, and in fo coftly a manner, cultivated; the number too of theatres, in all which the Gondoliers have admiffion gratis, may account for the fuperior manner in which they fing compared with people of the fame clafs elfewhere *. And in the private families, into which the girls of

* When a box belonging to a noble family is difengaged, and likely to remain empty, the opera manager permits the Gondolieri to occupy it, rather than a report fhould prevail that the performance drew but little company.

4

the

the Confervatorios marry, it is natural to
fuppofe that good tafte and a love for
mufic are introduced.

The library of St. Mark here, which
abounds with books in all other facul-
ties, afforded me but few materials on
the fubject of mufic. However I gained
confiderably by the converfation of Signor Zanetti, the firft librarian, who was
very polite and communicative.

Printing has been carried on in Venice
with great fpirit, ever fince the year 1459,
when it was eftablifhed there by Nicho-
las Janfen; and there is perhaps no
city in Italy in which fo many books
have been publifhed. At prefent the
prefs is very active and fertile, and the
number of bookfellers in the fine ftreet
called *Merceria* is very confiderable I
found in no one place fo many old authors on the fubject of mufic as here,
and as to the new, I met with many that
I was unable to find elfewhere, particularly the firft volume of Padre Martini's

Hiftory

History of Music. The principal bookfellers in Venice are Pafquali, Remondini,
Bettinelli, Occhi, and Antonio di Caftro.

The art of engraving mufic there feems
to be utterly loft, as I was not able to find
a fingle work printed in the manner we
print mufic in England. In the firft
place there is no fuch thing as a mufic
ftop throughout Italy, that I was able to
difcover. Indeed M. di Caftro, a fpirited
bookfeller, one of the four abovementioned, has publifhed a propofal for printing mufic with types, in the manner attempted by Mr. Fought, but has met
with fmall encouragement, having only
publifhed one book of little duets and
trios. Mufical compofitions are fo fhort-
lived in Italy, fuch is the rage for novelty, that for the few copies wanted, it is
not worth while to be at the expence of
engraving, and of the rolling-prefs. Indeed there, as in Turkey, the bufinefs of
a tranfcriber furnifhes employment for
fo many people, that it is cruel to wifh
to rob them of it, efpecially as that

trade

trade feems more brifk and profitable than any other.

As a fupplement to the article Venice, I muft add, that, fince my return to England, I have been favoured with a letter from thence, dated January 25, 1771, containing the following particulars relative to the ftate of mufic there, at that time. " At the theatre of S. Benetto we " have had reprefented, during the pre- " fent carnival, the opera of Alexander " in India ; compofed by Signor Bertoni, " mafter of the *Mendicanti,* which has " been univerfally applauded ; particu- " larly a duet, fung by Signora de Amicis " and Signor Cafelli. At the fame " theatre we have at prefent *il Siroe ri- " conofciuto,* compofed by Signor Borghi, " which is generally difliked.

" The mufic, at the opera-houfe of S. " Moisè, pleafes very much ; notwith- " ftanding it is fo ill executed, that the " author, Signor Garzaniga, a Neapoli- " tan, has great reafon to be mortified, " though crowned with general praife."

BOLOGNA.

BOLOGNA.

My chief errand in this city was to fee and converfe with the learned *Padre Martini*, and the celebrated Signor *Farinelli*, the former being regarded by all Europe as the deepeft theorift, and the other as the greateft practical mufician of this, or perhaps of any age or country; and, as I was fo fortunate as to be well received by both, I fhall make no apology for being minute in my account of two fuch extraordinary perfons.

Padre Martini is a Francifcan, and Maeftro di Capella of the church belonging to that order in Bologna. He has many years been employed in writing the Hiftory of Mufic, of which the firft volume only has, as yet, been publifhed. Two editions, one in folio, and one in quarto, were printed at the fame time in Bologna, 1757; a fecond volume is in the prefs, and he propofes finifhing the work in five volumes. The firft volume

is

is chiefly employed in the History of
Mufic among the Hebrews; the fecond
and third will comprife that of the ancient
Greeks; the fourth the Latin or
Roman mufic, with the hiftory of mufic
in the church; the fifth and laft volume
will be appropriated to modern
mufic, with fome account of the lives
and writings of the moft famous muficians, and engravings of their heads. We
reciprocally agreed upon an open and
cordial correfpondence, and a mutual promife of confidence and affiftance; but
it is greatly to be lamented that the good
Father Martini is far advanced in years,
and is of an infirm conftitution, having
a very bad cough, fwelled legs, and a
fickly countenance; fo that there is reafon to fear he will hardly have life and
health fufficient to complete his learned,
ingenious, and extenfive plan.

It is impoffible, by reading his book,
to form a judgment of the character of
this good and worthy man. As yet
he

he has treated only the driest and most abstruse part of the subject, in which he had great opportunities to shew his reading and knowledge, which are deep and extensive, but none to display the excellence of his character, which is such as inspires not only respect but kindness. He joins to innocence of life, and simplicity of manners, a native chearfulness, softness, and philanthropy. Upon so short an acquaintance I never liked any man more; and I felt as little reserve with him in a few hours, as with an old friend or beloved brother; it was impossible for confidence to be more cordial, especially between two persons whose pursuits were the same: it is however true, that though they are the same with respect to the object, they are different with respect to the way: I had advanced too far to retreat before I could procure his book, and when I had found it, my plan was so much digested as to render the adoption or imitation of any

O   other

other very inconvenient. Besides, as
every object may be approached by a
different route, it may also be seen in a
different point of view; two different
persons therefore may exhibit it with
equal truth, and yet with great diversity·
I shall avail myself of P. Martini's learning and materials, as I would of his spec-
tacles, I shall apply them to my subject,
as it appears to me, without changing my
situation; and shall neither implicitly
adopt his sentiments in doubtful points,
nor transcribe them where we agree.

Besides his immense collection of printed books, which has cost him upwards
of a thousand zechins, P. Martini is in
possession of what no money can purchase,
MSS. and copies of MSS. in the Vatican
and Ambrosian libraries, and in those of
Florence, Pisa, and other places, for
which he has had a faculty granted him by
the Pope, and particular permission from
others in power. He has ten different
copies of the famous Micrologus of
Guido

Guido Aretinus, and as many made from different manuscripts of John de Muris, with several other very ancient and valuable MSS. He has one room full of them, two other rooms are appropriated to the reception of printed books, of which he has all the several editions extant; and a fourth to practical music, of which he has likewife a prodigious quantity in MS. The number of his books amounts to seventeen thoufand volumes, and he is ftill encreafing it from all parts of the world*. He fhewed me feveral of his most curious books and MSS. upon which I communicated to him the catalogue of mine. He was furprifed at fome

---

* I had frequently furprifed feveral bookfellers on the continent with the lift of my books on the fubject of mufic, but, in my turn, I was now furprifed Though Padre Martini has had many prefents made him of fcarce books and MSS. yet he has often paid a great price for others, particularly for one written in Spanifh, 1613, which coft him a hundred ducats, about twenty guineas, at Naples, where it was printed.

of

of them, and faid they were extremely
rare; of thefe he took down the titles,
and, at my fecond vifit, he was pleafed to
think my plan worth borrowing to tranfcribe, which he did with his own
hand.

Thurfday, Auguft 23. It will give pleafure to every lover of mufic, efpecially
thofe who have been fo happy to have
heard him, that Signor Farinelli ftill
lives, and is in good health and fpirits.
I found him much younger in appearance
than I expected. He is tall and thin, but
by no means infirm in his appearance.
Hearing I had letter for him, he was fo
obliging as to come to me this morning at
Padre Martini's, in whofe library I fpent
a great part of my time here. Upon my
obferving, in the courfe of our converfation, that I had long been ambitious of
feeing two perfons, become fo eminent
by different abilities in the fame art, and
that my chief bufinefs at Bologna was to
gratify that ambition, Signor Farinelli,

point-

pointing to P. Martini, faid, "What *he*
" is doing will laft, but the little that I
" have done is already gone. and forgot-
" ten." I told him, that in England
there were ftill many who remembered
his performance fo well, that they could
bear to hear no other finger; that the
whole kingdom continued to refound his
fame, and I was fure tradition would
hand it down to the lateft pofterity.

Friday 24. This being St. Bartholo-
mew's day, I went to the church of that
name, where I was told the mufic would
be good; however, I found it quite the
contrary. Signor Gibello was *Maeftro di
Capella*, and feveral *caftrati* fung, but
neither the compofition nor execution
pleafed me; the compofition had not one
of Buranello's three requifites, *vaghezza,
chiarezza, e buona modulazione*, to recommend it, and the execution was flovenly and incorrect.

Though there was no opera in Bologna
at this time, yet, for the fake of feeing

the

the theatre, I went to the play. The
houſe is elegant, but not large; it has
however five rows of boxes, twelve or
thirteen on a ſide. When I went in I
knew not what the play would be, but
expeӝed a ribbald farce, as uſual; when,
to my great ſurpriſe, I found it was an
Italian tragedy, called *Tomire*, written by
Padre Ringhieri. I had never ſeen one
before, and was much pleaſed with the
opening, but ſoon grew tired of the long
ſpeeches and declamation; they were
paſt all bearing tedious. Thomyris,
Queen of the Amazons, came on dreſſed
in a very equivocal manner; for, in order to give her a martial look, ſhe had
her petticoats truſſed up in front above
her knees, which were very diſcernible
through her black breeches. However
ſtrange this appeared to me, the audience
clapped violently, as they did conſtantly
at the worſt and moſt abſurd things in
the piece. There was a great deal of
religion in it, and ſuch anachroniſms,
that

that they talked of J. C. and the Trinity, nor were Free-will and Predeſtination forgotten, and when Cyrus is dying of the wound he received in battle, he is examined by a Jewiſh prieſt (a principal character in the play) as his confeſſor, concerning his religious principles, and he makes to him a *profeſſion of faith.*

This kind of ſpectacle has been ſo long neglected in Italy, that it ſeems to have been wholly loſt; and now, after a ſecond birth, appears to be in its *infancy.* However, the Italian language is certainly capable of great things; as it can ſupport dignity without the trammels of rhyme. The actors too are good, as to propriety and variety of geſture; but in voice, a monotony reigns here, as in the Italian pulpit. The paſſion for dramas in muſic has ruined true tragedy as well as comedy in this country; but the language and genius of the people are ſo rich and fertile, that when they become heartily tired of muſic, which by exceſs of it they

O 4   will

will probably be very foon, the fame rage
for novelty, which has made them fly with
fuch rapidity from one ftile of compofition to another, often changing from a
better to a worfe, will drive them to feek
amufement from the ftage, *without* mufic.
And in that cafe, when they apply all
their powers to the fock and bufkin, and
the writer and actor are obliged to make
ufe of every refource with which the national language and genius abound; they
will probably furpafs the reft of Europe
in the dramatic, as well as in other arts:
But before this can happen, much muft
be done towards refining the national
tafte, which is at prefent too much depraved by farce, buffoonery, and fong.
The inattention, noife, and indecorum
of the audience too, are quite barbarous
and intolerable The filence which reigns
in the theatres of London and Paris,
during reprefentation, is encouraging to
the actor, as well as defirable to the hearer of judgment and feeling. In Italy
the

the theatres are immenfe, and, in order to
be heard through fpace and noife, the
actors feem in a perpetual bawl. Each
fentence, thus pronounced, is more like
the harangue of a general at the head
of an army of a hundred thoufand men,
than the fpeech of a hero or heroine in
converfation; this allows of but few
modulations of voice; all the paffions
are alike noify, the tender and the tur-
bulent.

The fcenes and decorations in this
piece were elegant and judicious; there
was one fcene in particular very ftriking;
it was that of a high, but fertile moun-
tain, from which Thomyris defcended
with her court and guards, in order to
come to a parley with Cyrus.

The orcheftra was rather weak and ordinary; and, in general, I found the mufic
in the ftreets here worfe, and lefs frequent
then at Venice. However, I was faluted
foon after my arrival at the inn, as every
ftranger is, with a duet, very well played
by

by a violin and mandoline; and, this afternoon, an itinerant band played under my window feveral fymphonies and fingle movements of execution, extremely well, in four parts.

Saturday 25. This day I had the pleafure to fpend with Signor Farinelli, at his houfe in the country, about a mile from Bologna, which is not yet quite finifhed, though he has been building it ever fince he retired from Spain *. Il Padre Maeftro Martini was invited to dine there with me, and I cannot refift the defire of confeffing that I was extremely happy at finding myfelf in the company of two fuch extraordinary men.

Signor Farinelli has long left off finging, but amufes himfelf ftill on the harp-

* The country is flat all round him, but though the environs of this city are perhaps the moft fertile of any in Italy, yet the inhabitants feem poffeffed of nothing like *tafte*, in laying out their gardens, however, Signor Farinelli's houfe commands a fine profpect of Bologna, and of the little hills near it.

4   fichord

fichord and viol d' amour: he has a great number of harpfichords made in different countries, which he has named according to the place they hold in his favour, after the gieateft of the Italian painters. His firft favourite is a *piano forte*, made at Florence in the year 1730, on which is written in gold letters, *Rafael d'Urbino*; then, Coreggio, Titian, Guido, &c. He played a confiderable time upon this Raphael, with great judgment and delicacy, and has compofed feveral elegant pieces for that inftrument. The next in favour is a harpficord given him by the late queen of Spain, who was Scarlatti's fcholar, both in Portugal and Spain; it was for this princefs that Scarlatti made his two firft books of leffons, and to her the firft edition, printed at Venice, was dedicated, when fhe was princefs of Afturias: this harpfichord, which was made in Spain, has more tone than any of the others. His third favourite is one made

likewife

likewife in Spain, under his own direction; it has moveable keys, by which,
like that of Count Taxis, at Venice, the
player can tranfpofe a compofition either
higher or lower. Of thefe Spanifh harpfichords the natural keys are black, and
the flats and fharps are covered with mother of pearl; they are of the Italian
model, all the wood is cedar, except the
bellies, and they are put into a fecond
cafe.

Signor Farinelli was very converfible
and communicative, and talked over old
times very freely, particularly thofe when
he was in England; and I am inclined
to believe, that his life, were it well
written, would be very interefting to the
public, as it has been much chequered,
and fpent in the firft courts of Europe;
but, as I hope it is yet far from finifhed,
this feems not to be the place to attempt
it: however, the following anecdotes,
chiefly picked up in converfation with
himfelf

himfelf and Padre Martini, may perhaps for the prefent, gratify in fome meafure, the curiofity of the reader.

Carlo Brofchi, called Farinelli, was born at Naples in 1705, he had his firft mufical education from his father, Signor Brofchi, and afterwards was under Porpora, who travelled with him, he was feventeen when he left that city to go to Rome, where, during the run of an opera, there was a ftruggle every night between him and a famous player on the trumpet, in a fong accompanied by that inftrument. this, at firft, feemed amicable and merely fportive, till the audience began to intereft themfelves in the conteft, and to take different fides: After feverally fwelling out a note, in which each manifefted the power of his lungs, and tried to rival the other in brilliancy and force, they had both a fwell and a fhake together, by thirds, which was continued fo long, while the audience eagerly waited the event, that both

both feemed to be exhaufted, and, in fact, the trumpeter, wholly fpent, gave it up, thinking, however, his antagonift as much tired as himfelf, and that it would be a drawn battle, when Farinelli, with a fmile on his countenance, fhewing he had only been fporting with him all this time, broke out all at once in the fame breath, with frefh vigour, and not only fwelled and fhook the note, but ran the moft rapid and difficult divifions, and was at laft filenced only by the acclamations of the audience. From this period may be dated that fuperiority which he ever maintained over all his cotemporaries.

In the early part of his life he was diftinguifhed throughout Italy, by the name of *the boy*.

From Rome he went to Bologna, where he had the advantage of hearing Bernacchi, (a fcholar of the famous Piftocco, of that city) who was then the

firft

firſt finger in Italy, for taſte and knowledge; and his ſcholars afterwards rendered the Bologna ſchool famous.

From thence he went to Venice, and
from Venice to Vienna; in all which
cities his powers were regarded as miraculous; but he told me, that at Vienna,
where he was three different times, and
where he received great honours from
the Emperor Charles the VI. an admo-
nition from that prince was of more
ſervice to him than all the precepts of his
maſters, or examples of his competitors
for fame: his Imperial Majeſty conde-
ſcended to tell him one day, with great
mildneſs and affability, that in his ſinging, he neither *moved* nor *ſtood ſtill* like
any other mortal; all was ſupernatural.
" Thoſe gigantic ſtrides, (ſaid he); thoſe
" never-ending notes and paſſages *(ces*
" *notes qui ne finiſſent jamais)* only ſur-
" priſe, and it is now time for you to
" pleaſe; you are too laviſh of the gifts
" with which nature has endowed you;
" if

" if you wish to reach the heart, you
" must take a more plain and simple
" road." These few words brought a-
bout an entire change in his manner of
singing; from this time he mixed the
pathetic with the spirited, the simple
with the sublime, and, by these means,
delighted as well as astonished every
hearer.

In the year 1734, he came into England, where every one knows who heard,
or has heard of him, what an effect his
surprising talents had upon the audience:
it was extacy! rapture! enchantment!

In the famous air *Son qual Nave*, which
was composed by his brother, the first
note he sung was taken with such delicacy, swelled by minute degrees to such
an amazing volume, and afterwards di-
minished in the same manner, that it was
applauded for full five minutes. He afterwards set off with such brilliancy and
rapidity of execution, that it was difficult
for the violins of those days to keep pace

6   with

with him. In fhort, he was to all other
fingers as fuperiour as the famous horfe
Childers was to all other runring-horfes;
but it was not only in fpeed, he had now
every excellence of every great finger
united. In his voice, ftrength, fweetnefs,
and compafs; in his ftile, the tender, the
graceful, and the rapid. He poffeffed
fuch powers as never met before, or fince,
in any one human being; powers that
were irrefiftible, and which muft fubdue
every hearer; the learned and the ignorant, the friend and the foe.

With thefe talents he went into Spain
in the year 1737, with a full defign to
return into England, having entered into
articles with the nobility, who had then
the management of the opera, to perform
the enfuing feafon. In his way thither
he fung to the king of France at Paris,
where, according to Riccoboni, he enchanted even the French themfelves, who
at that time univerfally abhorred Italian
mufic; but the firft day he performed

before the king and queen of Spain, it was determined that he fhould be taken into the fervice of the court, to which he was ever after wholly appropriated, not being once fuffered to fing again in public. A penfion was then fettled on him of upwards of 2000 l. fterling a year.

He told me, that for the firft ten years of his refidence at the court of Spain, during the life of Philip the Vth, he fung every night to that monarch the fame four airs, of which two were compofed by Haffe, *Pal·do il fole*, and *Per quéfto dolce Ampleffo*. I forget the others, but one was a minuet which he ufed to vary at his pleafure.

After the death of Philip the Vth, his favour continued under his fucceffor Ferdinand the VIth, by whom he was dignified with the order of *Calatrava* in 1750; but then his duty became lefs conftant and fatiguing, as he perfuaded this prince to have operas, which were a

great

great relief to him : he was appointed sole director of thofe fpectacles ; and had from Italy, the beft compofers and fingers of the time, and Metaftafio to write. He fhewed me in his houfe four of the principal fcenes in *Didone* and *Netette*, painted by Amiconi, who accompanied him firft into England, and then into Spain, where he died.

When the prefent king of Spain afcended the throne, he was obliged to quit that kingdom, but his penfion is ftill continued, and he was allowed to bring away all his effects. The furniture of his houfe is very rich, as it is almoft entirely compofed of the prefents he received from great perfonages. He feems very much to regret the being obliged to feek a new habitation, after having lived twenty-four years in Spain, where he had formed many friendfhips and connections that were dear to him ; and it is a great proof of the prudence and moderation of his character, that in a country and court,

P 2   where

where jealousy and pride are so predomi-
nant, he continued so long to be the king's
chief favourite, a distinction odious to
every people, without the least quarrel or
difference with any of the Spaniards.

When he returned into Italy in 1761,
all his old friends, relations, and acquaintance were either dead or removed
from the places where he had left them,
so that he had a second life to begin,
without the charms of youth to attach
new friends, or his former talents to gain
new protectors.

He says that Metastasio and he were
twins of public favour, and entered the
world at the same time, he having performed in that poet's first opera. When
he shewed me his house, he pointed out
an original picture, painted about that
time, by Amiconi, in which are the port-
raits of Metastasio, of Farinelli himself,
of Faustina, the famous singer, and of
Amiconi.

From

From his conversation, there is reason
to believe, that the court of Spain had
fixed on Bologna for his residence; though
the Italians say his first design was to
settle at Naples, the place of his birth,
but that he was driven from thence by
the numerous and importunate claims of
his relations: however that may be, he
has a sister and two of her children with
him, one of whom is an infant, of which
he is doatingly fond, though it is cross,
sickly, homely, and unamiable; yet this
is a convincing proof, among others, to me
that he was designed by nature for family
attentions, and domestic comforts: but in
conversation he lamented his not being
able, for political reasons, to settle in
England; for, next to Spain, that was
the place in the world, he said, where he
should have wished to spend the remain-
der of his days.

He speaks much of the respect and gratitude he owes to the English. When I
dined with him it was on an elegant ser-

vice

vice of plate, made in England at the time he was there. He shewed me a number of pictures of himself, painted during that time, from one of which by Amiconi, there is a print. He has an English sweep chimney boy playing with a cat, and an apple-woman with a barrow, by the same hand: he has likewise a curious English clock, with little figures playing in concert on the guitar, the violin, and violoncello, whose arms and fingers are always moved by the same pendulum.

His large room, in which is a billiard-table, is furnished with the pictures of great personages, chiefly sovereign princes, who have been his patrons, among whom are two emperors, one emprefs, three kings of Spain, two princes of Afturias, a king of Sardinia, a prince of Savoy, a king of Naples, a princefs of Afturias, two queens of Spain, and Pope Benedict the XIVth. In other apartments are several charming pictures, by Zimenes and Morillo,

rillo, two Spanish painters of the first eminence, and Spagnolet.

Sir Benjamin Keene was a great favourite with him, and he speaks of his death, not only as a misfortune to the two courts of England and Spain, but as an irreparable loss to himself and all his friends. He shewed me several pictures painted in England, in the manner of Teniers, by a man, during the time he was in prison for debt, I forget his name; these, he said, Lord Chesterfield had given him in the politest manner imaginable.

Upon my expressing some desire to write his life, or, at least, to insert particulars of it in my history. " Ah," says he, by a modesty rather pushed too far, " if you have a mind to compose a good " work, never fill it with accounts of such " despicable beings as I am." However, he furnished me with all the particulars concerning Domenico Scarlatti, which I desired, and dictated to me very oblig-

ingly,

ingly, while I entered them in my pocket-book.

He still retains a few words of the English language, which he had picked up during his refidence in London, and entertained me a great part of the day with accounts of his reception and adventures there. He repeated a converfation he had with Queen Caroline, about Cuzzoni and Fauftina, and gave me an account of his firft performance at court to his late majefty George the IId. in which he was accompanied on the harpfichord by the princefs royal, afterwards princefs of Orange, who infifted on his finging two of Handel's fongs at fight, printed in a different clef, and compofed in a different ftile from what he had ever been ufed to. He told me of his journey into the country with the Duke and Duchefs of Leeds; and with Lord Cobham; of the feuds of the two operas; of the part which the late Prince of Wales took with that managed by the nobility; and the Queen

and

and Princefs Royal with that which was under the direction of Handel.

He likewife confirmed to me the truth of the following extraordinary ftory, which I had often heard, but never before credited. Senefino and Farinelli, when in England together, being engaged at different theatres on the fame night, had not an opportunity of hearing each other, till, by one of thofe fudden ftage-revolutions which frequently happen, yet are always unexpected, they were both employed to fing on the fame ftage. Senefino had the part of a furious tyrant to reprefent, and Farinelli that of an unfortunate hero in chains; but, in the courfe of the firft fong, he fo foftened the obdurate heart of the enraged tyrant, that Senefino, forgetting his ftage-character, ran to Farinelli and embraced him in his own.

Monday 22. This day, after vifiting the Inftitute, I waited on the *Dottoreffa Madame Laura Baffi*, and met with a very
polite

polite and eafy reception. Upon naming
Padre Beccaria, and fhewing his recommendation in my tablets, we were inftantly good friends. This lady is between
fifty and fixty; but though learned, and
a genius, not at all mafculine or affum-
ing. We talked over the moft celebrated
men of fcience in Europe. She was very
civil to the Englifh, in eulogiums of
Newton, Halley, Bradley, Franklin, and
others. She fhewed me her electrical
machine and apparatus. the machine is
fimple, portable, and convenient; it confifts of a plain plate of glafs, placed ver-
tically, the two cufhions are covered
with red leather, the receiver is a tin
forked tube; the two forks, with pins at
the ends, are placed next the glafs plate.
She is very dextrous and ingenious in her experiments, of which fhe was fo obliging as
to fhew me feveral She told me that Signor
Bafii, her hufband, immediately after Dr.
Franklin had proved the identity of electrical fire and lightning, and publifhed

I   his

his method of preferving buildings from the effects of it, by iron rods, had caufed conductors to be erected at the Inftitute; but that the people of Bologna were fo afraid of the rods, believing they would bring the lightning upon them, inftead of the contrary, that he was forced to take them down. Benedict XIV. one of the moft enlightened and enlarged of the popes, a native, and in a particular manner the patron, as well as fovereign of Bologna, wrote a letter to recommend the ufe of thefe conductors; but it was fo much againft the inclination of the inhabitants of this city, that Signor Baffi defifted entirely, and they have never fince that time been ufed here.

There is an apparatus, and a room apart for electricity at the Inftitute, but the machines are old, and very inferior to thofe in ufe at this time in England. It is remarkable that this univerfity has no correfpondence with England, nor is it able to purchafe our Phi-

lofophical

lofophical Tranfactions. The falaries
are fmall, and the money allowed for the
fupport of the Inftitute is all appropriated. This I was told by the Keeper
or *Cuftode*, who fhewed me the apartments. My vifit with the learned Signora Baffi was very agreeable, and fhe
was fo obliging as to offer me a letter to
Signor Fontana at Florence, one of the
firft mathematicians in Europe.

They fpeak much at Bologna of the
Brav' Orbi, or blind fidlers, who were
not in town when I was there; but all
the mafters admire them, in their way,
very much, particularly Iomelli, who
always fends for them, when in the fame
town, to play to him. They travel
about in fummer to Rome, Naples, and
elfewhere: one plays on the violin, the
other on the violoncello, and is called
Spacca Nota, or Split Note.

Tuefday being a feftival, mafs was
performed in mufic at the church of the
convent of St Auguftin The compofer
was

was Signor Caroli, *Maeftro di Capella del Duomo* of Bologna. There was a great band, but neither learning, tafte, or novelty to recommend the mufic. It confifted of old paffages, ftrung together in a heavy manner, without even the merit of a little pertnefs now and then to enliven it. And what rendered this mufic ftill more tirefome, was the finging, which was rather below mediocrity.

In the afternoon I went to take a melancholy leave of the Cavalier Farinelli. He kindly importuned me to ftay longer at Bologna, and even chid me for going away fo foon. I found him at his Raphael, and prevailed on him to play a good deal: he *fings* upon it with infinite tafte and expreffion. I was truly forry to quit this extraordinary and amiable perfon : he preffed me to write to him, if there was any thing in Italy which he could procure or do for me. I ftaid with him till it was fo late, that I was in danger of being fhut out of the city of Bologna, the gates being

ing locked every night as foon as it is dark.

By the advice of P. Martini I ſtaid at Bologna two days longer than I intended, in order to be preſent at a kind of trial of ſkill among ſuch compoſers of this city as are members of the celebrated Philharmonic Society, founded in 1666.

There is an annual exhibition, or public performance, morning and evening, on the thirtieth of Auguſt, in the church of *S. Johanni in Monte* *. This year the *Principe*, or Preſident, was Signor Petronio Lanzi. The band was very numerous, confiſting of near a hundred voices and inſtruments. There are two large organs in the church, one on each ſide

* This church is rendered famous by the poſſeſſion of two of the beſt pictures in Bologna, or, perhaps, in the world, the St Cecilia of Raphael, and the Madonna of the Roſary of Dominichini. They are placed in two chapels, oppoſite to each other, between which, and in full view of theſe charming paintings, I had the advantage of ſitting to hear the muſic

of

of the choir; and, besides these, a small one was erected for the occasion, in front, just behind the composer and singers. The performers were placed in a gallery, which formed a semi-circle round the choir

In the *Messa* or Morning Service the *Kyrie* and *Gloria* were composed by Signor Lanzi, President for the second time. His music was grave and majestic; it opened with an introduction, by way of overture, of a considerable length, which afterwards served as an accompaniment to the voices in a very good chorus: there were likewise in it several pleasing airs, and a well-written fugue.

The *Graduale* was composed by Signor Antonio Caroli, in the same dry, uninteresting stile as the performance mentioned above, which would have been thought trite and dull sixty years ago.

The *Credo* was composed by Signor Lorenzo Gibelli, a scholar of Padre Martini,

tini, which, in point of harmony, h
its merit.

The morning service was finished by a
symphony, with solo parts, by Signor
Gioanni Piantanida, principal violin of
Bologna, which really aftonished me.
This performer is upwards of fixty years
of age, and yet has all the fire of youth,
with a good tone, and modern tafte; and,
upon the whole, feemed to me, (though
his bow-hand has a clumfy and aukward
look) more powerful upon his inftrument
than any one I had, as yet, heard in
Italy.

In the *Vefpero*, or evening fervice, the
Domine was compofed by Signor Anto.
Fontana di Carpi, a prieft, and was a
pleafing performance, of one movement
only.

The Abate Gio. Califto Zanotti, nephew to the learned librarian of that
name, compofed the *Dixit*; and in this
performance there were all the marks of
an original and cultivated genius. The
move-

Movements, and even paffages were well contrafted ; and, to make ufe of the language of painters, there were difcernible in it, not only light and fhade, but even *mezzo tints*. He proceeded from one thing to another by fuch eafy and infenfible gradations, that it feemed wholly the work of nature, though conducted with the greateft art. The accompaniments were judicious, the ritornels always expreffed *fomething*, the melody was new and full of tafte, and the whole was put together with great judgment, and even learning. In fhort, I have very feldom in my life received greater pleafure from mufic than this performance afforded me ; and yet the vocal parts were but indifferently executed, for at this time there were no great fingers at Bologna, though there were two or three that were agreeable, particularly a *contr' alto*, Signor Cicognani, who, in a ferious opera, would be a good fecond finger ; and a *foprano*, Confoli, a boy of about thirteen

Q

or fourteen, with a very fweet, but feeble voice, who poffeffed great tafte and expreffion. Signor Zanotti is a fcholar of Padre Martini, and one of the *Maeftri di Capella* in the church of S. Petronio.

The next compofer who took upon him the direction of the orcheftra (every author beat time to his own performance) was Signor Gabrielle Vignali. His part of the fervice was the *Confitebor*, which he had fet in fuch an inoffenfive manner, that the niceft judge could not be hurt by its faults, nor the moft envious critic by its beauties.

Beatus Vir was fet by D. Giufeppe Coretti, a venerable prieft, who ranks very high in Bologna as a *contrapuntift*; indeed his mufic was very mafterly, and, in found harmony, and regular modulation, had infinite merit.

Laudato Puer was compofed by Signor Bernardo Ottani, another fcholar of P. Martini, who is young, and a promifing compofer. There were many ingenious

pretty

pretty things in his performance, as well as in that which followed, which was a hymn by D. Francefco Orfoni, a young prieft, and fcholar likewife of P. Martini.

The whole was concluded by the *Magnificat* of Signor Antonio Mazzoni, fecond mafter of the *duomo* or cathedral, who is compofer to the opera here, and has been in that character at Naples, Madrid, and Peterfbourg. He is faid to have great fire and fancy, but in this performance, which was all chorus, they were not difcoverable; the whole was founded upon a ground-bafe, which was played by all the inftruments, and feemed laboured and conftrained.

There were prefent at this exhibition all the critics of Bologna, and the neighbouring cities, and the church was extremely crowded. Upon the whole, I was very well entertained; and the variety of ftile, and mafterly compofition were fuch as reflected honour, not only

upon

upon the Philharmonic Society, but upon the city of Bologna itfelf, which has, at all times, been fertile in genius, and has given birth to a great number of men of abilities in all the arts.

I muft acquaint my mufical reader, that at the performance juft mentioned, I met with M. Mozart and his fon, the little German, whofe premature and almoft fupernatural talents aftonifhed us in London a few years ago, when he had fcarce quitted his infant ftate. Since his arrival in Italy he has been much admired at Rome and Naples; has been honoured with the order of the *Speron d'Oro*, or Golden Spur, by his Holinefs, and was engaged to compofe an opera at Milan for the next Carnival.

I cannot quit this city without returning once more to the good Padre Martini. After the mufical performance above defcribed, I went, by appointment, to his convent to bid him adieu, as I was to quit Bologna early next morning. He

waited

waited for me in his ſtudy, it being late, and beyond the monaſtic hours of ſeeing company. He had kindly prepared for me recommendatory letters for Florence, Rome, and Naples; and had looked out ſtill more curious books to ſhew me, of which I took the titles, in hopes of meeting with them ſome time or other. He had told me, the day before, that, as he ſhould not be preſent at the Philharmonic Meeting, he ſhould rely on my judgment and account, how matters went off and were conducted; and now deſired me to deſcribe to him every ſingle piece. After doing this very faithfully, I was going to retire, when he ſays, " Won't you ſtay " for the words to be written to theſe " Canons ?"—I had the day before ſung with a young Franciſcan, his ſcholar, out of a prodigous large MS. book of his Canons, ſeveral very pleaſing ones for two voices only, of which I ſeemed to expreſs a deſire to have one or two copied, and this excellent father remem-

bering

bering it, had set a person to work for me, who was writing when I entered the study; but, as he had usually two or three *amanuenses* there, I did not mind him *. At length we parted, on my side with sorrow, and on his with a recommendation to write to him often.

FLORENCE.

This city has been longer in possession of music, if the poets and historians may be credited, than any other in Europe. Dante, a Florentine, born in 1265, speaks of the organ and lute as instruments well known in his time; and has taken an opportunity to celebrate the talents of his friend Casella, the musician, in the second canto of his *Purgatorio*.

The historian Villani, cotemporary with Petrarca, says that his *canzonets* were

---

* Padre Martini has composed an amazing number of ingenious and learned *canons*, in which every kind of intricacy and contrivance, that ever had admission into this difficult species of composition, has been happily subdued.

uni-

univerfally fung in Florence, by the old
and the young of both fexes. And we
are told that *Lorenzo il Magnifico*, in
Carnival time, ufed to go out in the evening, followed by a numerous company
of perfons on horfeback, mafked, and
richly dreffed, amounting fometimes to
upwards of three hundred; and the fame
number on foot, with wax tapers burning, which rendered the ftreets as light
as at noon day, and gave a fplendour to
the whole fpectacle. In this manner
they marched through the city, till three
or four o'clock in the morning, finging,
with *mufical harmony*, in four, eight,
twelve, and even fifteen parts, accompanied with various inftruments, fongs,
ballads, madrigals, and catches, or fongs
of humour, upon fubjects then in vogue;
and thefe, from being performed in Carnival time, were called *Canti Carnafcia-*
lefchi. *

* They were firft collected and publifhed by
Francefco Spaziano Florence, 1559.

But

But even before this period the company of *Laudifi*, or Pfalm-fingers, was formed, which has continued ever fince; it is now called *La Compagnia*, and the morning after my arrival in Florence, between fix and feven o'clock, they paffed by the inn where I lodged, in grand proceffion, dreffed in a whitifh uniform, with burning tapers in their hands. They ftopped at the *duomo*, or great church, juft by, to fing a chearful hymn, in three parts, which they executed very well. In this manner, on Sundays and holidays, the trades-people and artifans form themfelves into diftinct companies, and fing through the ftreets, in their way to church. Thofe of the parifh of S. Benedetto, we are informed by Crefcimbeni, were famous all over Italy; and at the great Jubilee, in the beginning of this century, marched through the ftreets of Rome, finging in fuch a manner as pleafed and aftonifhed every body.

September

September 13. I went to the little theatre *di via Santa Maria*, to hear the comic opera of *La Pescatrice*, composed by Signor Piccini. There are but four characters in this drama, two of which were represented by Signora Giovanna Baglioni, and her sister Costanza, whom I had heard at Milan; the other two were Signor Paolo Bonaveri, a good tenor, and Signor Gostantino Ghigi. Giov. Baglioni appeared here to much greater advantage than at Milan, where the theatre is of such a size as to require the lungs of a Stentor to fill it. She sung very well, her voice is clear, and always in tune, her shake open and perfect, and her taste and expression left nothing to wish in the songs she had to sing. She was extremely applauded; the house was very much crowded, the band was good, and the music worthy of Signor Piccini; full of that fire and fancy which characterise all the productions of that ingenious and original composer.

In.

In the duomo, or cathedral here, which is one of the largeſt churches in Italy, there is the fineſt toned organ I ever heard; whether, like St. Paul's, in London, it is meliorated by the magnitude and happy conſtruction of the building, I cannot tell, but it pleaſed me exceedingly. It has moreover, the advantage of being very well played on by Signor Matucci, the preſent organiſt, whoſe ſtile is not only grave and ſuitable to the church, but learned in modulation, and, in ſlow move-ments, truly pathetic.

M. de Maupertuis, in his voyage to the polar circle, was told by the Laplanders of a monument which they regarded as the moſt wonderful thing in their coun-try: upon the merits of this report only, he ſays, he was almoſt aſhamed to confeſs that he undertook a very fatiguing and dangerous journey to ſee it. Something of the ſame kind happened to me: in go-ing to the opera, a ſecond time, I was ſur-prized to find the theatre almoſt empty;
and,

and, upon enquiry into the reason of it, I
was told that the chief muficians, and
the beft company of Italy, were affembled
at Fighne, a town in the Upper Val
d'Arno, about thirty miles from Florence,
to celebrate a kind of jubilee, in honour
of Santa Maffimina, the protectrefs of that
place; and I am almoft afhamed to confefs, that, without enquiring of perfons
well informed, I took upon truft this report, and travelled all night, in order to
be prefent at thefe games the next day.

I arrived at the place of action about
feven o'clock in the morning, and found
the road and town very full of country
people, as at a wake in England, but faw
very few carriages, or perfons of rank and
fafhion; however, confiderable prepara-
tions were making in the great fquare,
for the diverfions of the evening.

At eleven high mafs was performed in
the principal church, which was very
much ornamented, and illuminated with
innumerable

innumerable wax tapers, which, together with the greatest crowd I ever was in, rendered the heat almost equal to that of the black-hole at Calcutta, and the confequences muft have been as fatal, had not the people been permitted to go out as others preffed in ; but neither religious zeal, nor the love of mufic, could keep any one long in the church who was able to get out. In fhort, the whole was a ftruggle between thofe whofe curiofity made them ftrive to enter the church, and others whofe fufferings and fear made them ufe every means in their power to get out.

By permitting myfelf to drive with the ftream, I at length was carried to a tolerable place near one of the doors, where I had perfeverance fufficient to remain during the whole fervice, as I was in conftant expectation of being rewarded for my fufferings, by the performance of fome great finger, whom I had not heard before ;

fore, but in this I was difappointed, as all the vocal performers, except one *, were very indifferent: the mufic, however, was very pretty; full of tafte and fancy: it was compofed by Signor Feroce, Fiorentino. The principal violin was played by Signor Modele, who, with his fon, played very neatly a duet concerto: after this the Abate Fibbietti fung a motet with fuch tafte in the flow movements, and fire in the quick, as were truly aftonifhing; his voice was fweet and clear, his intonations perfectly true; his expreffion and fancy charming, and he left nothing to wifh, but a fhake a little more open.

At four o'clock in the evening, the games began in the great fquare, which is a large piece of ground of an oblong form There were 1500 peafants of the neighbourhood employed upon this occafion, who had been three months in train-

---

* The Abate Fibbietti, an excellent tenor.

ing:

ing: they had the story of David and Goliah to reprefent, which was done with the moft minute attention to the facred ftory, and the *coftume* of the ancients. The two armies of the Ifraelites and Philiftines met, marching to the found of ancient inftruments, fuch as the *crotola* or cymbal, the fyftrum, and others: they were all dreffed *à l'Antique*, even to the common men; the kings, princes, and generals, on both fides, were fumptuoufly clad, and all on horfeback, as were feveral hundreds of the troops.

The giant, Goliah, advanced and gave the challenge: the Ifraelites retreated in great confternation, till, at length, little David appears, and entreats Saul to let him be his champion, which requeft, after fome time is granted; the reft of the ftory was well told, and it was fo contrived, that after Goliah was ftunned by the ftone from David's fling, in cutting off his head with the Giant's own great fword, a quantity of blood gufhed out, and many of

of the spectators shrieked with horror,
supposing it to be the blood of the person
who represented the champion of the
Philistines. After this, there was a
pitched battle between the two armies,
and the Israelites, being victorious, brought
David in triumph, at the head of the
prisoners and spoils of the enemy, mounted on a superb chariot, in the ancient
form,

At Vespers I heard the same story *sung*
in an oratorio, set by the Abate Ferocc,
in which Signor Fibbietti, the tenor, had
a capital part, to which he did great juftice. during this performance, the whole
town was illuminated in an elegant manner, and there were very ingenious fire-
works played off *in the great square;* and,
in justice to the pacific disposition of the
Tuscans, I must observe, that though
there were at least 20,000 people assem-
bled together on this occasion, without
guards, yet not the least accident or dif-
turbance happened. This may perhaps
be

be owing, in some measure, to the peculiar sobriety of the Italians, as I do not remember to have seen one drunken person during the whole time I was in Italy.

It being impossible to procure a bed, if I would have paid eight or ten zechins for it, and the night being very fine, I set out at eleven o'clock for Florence, where I arrived at four the next morning: and though the musical performance at Figline was not what I had been made to expect, yet the rest was very superior, and what I was not likely to meet with elsewhere; so that, upon the whole, I did not think the time spent in this excursion entirely lost.

Wednesday, Sept. 6. I was present at the performance of another opera, set by Piccini, called *Le Donne Vendicate.* There were in this drama but four characters, which were represented very well by the same persons as those in the *Pescatrice.* There are but two acts in any of the comic

mic operas I have yet feen in Italy; but the dances, which are likewife two, may be called *balli pantomimi,* or pantomime entertainments, as they are each as long almoft as an act of the opera. There are two or three charming airs in this burletta. Coftanza Baglioni fung extremely well; and the tenor, who is a favourite here, was very much applauded; but though a good finger, I neither think his voice or tafte equal to thofe of Signor Lovatini.

Friday, Sept. 7. In the evening I heard vefpers performed at the church of the Annunciation; by a great number of fingers, priefts and laymen, accompanied only by a little organ, a violoncello, and two double bafes. The mufic was in the old choral ftile of the fixteenth century. After this *full* performance, in the great choir, there was other finging in different chapels of this beautiful church, by boys placed in different organ lofts, who were

R   accompanied

accompanied by tenor and bafe voices below.

- *Saturday, Sept.* 8. This morning, there
were no other inftruments to accompany
the voices than thofe which I had heard
at the fame church yefterday, though the
day was a great feftival : however, the
vocal performers were more numerous,
and they fung a mafs in eight parts, four
on a fide, very well , it was compofed
by Orazio Benevoli, of the Roman fchool,
who flourifhed foon after Paleftrina, and,
for that time, and that kind of mufic, is
excellent.   There are no regular fugues,
the fubjects are changed with the words,
and little or no effect is produced by the
melody, when divided among fo many
parts; but the points and imitations *muft*
be fhort, or the movement would be end-
lefs   However, the effect of the *whole,*
to lovers of harmony, is admirable.   After the fervices were ended, Signor Veroli,
a very good foprano, fung a grave motet

I   *a voce*

a voce sola. He is usually the first singer in the serious opera here, and has a very pleasing voice, with a considerable share of taste. The motet was composed by Padre Dreyer, *Maestro di Capella* of the *Annunciata.* He was formerly a famous singer at Dresden, with a *soprano* voice, but on account of the too great notice which was taken of him, by a person of distinction there, he was sent away, and has been many years established in this city: he is now in years; I had a long conversation with him, and found him very intelligent and obliging. He says, the music of Palestrina is used here on all days, except festivals; and, upon my requesting him to favour me with a copy of the most celebrated composition performed in his church, he told me that it was the *Miserere* of *Allegri*, which is sung here, as in the Pope's chapel, only on Good Fridays, and that it should be transcribed for me immediately. but as I had already obtained a copy of that fa-

mous

mous compofition from Padre Martini, who had one made by the exprefs order of the late Pope, I declined the acceptance of his obliging offer.

In the evening I went again to the opera of *Le Donne Vendicate*, which I mention only becaufe it gives me an opportunity of remarking the extraordinary good humour of an Italian audience; for this being the laft night of the prefent company's performance, the crowd and applaufe were prodigious; printed fonnets, in praife of fingers and dancers, were thrown from the flips, and feen flying about the houfe in great numbers, for which the audience fcrambled with much eagernefs, and at the clofe of all, it was rather acclamation than applaufe.

Sunday, Sept. 9. This morning I was at a very folemn fervice in the convent *delle Monache*, or nuns of the *Portico*, about a mile from Florence. This performance coft upwards of 300 zechins,

it

it was the laft confecration of eight nuns ; the archbifhop was there, a great deal of the firft company of Florence, and a very numerous band of vocal and inftrumental performers. I had here the pleafure of hearing Signor Manzoli. In the firft part of the mafs, there was a trio between him, Signor Veroli, and the fecond *maeftro* of the Nunziata, whofe voice is a Baritono. The mufic of the mafs was by Signor Soffi, of Lucca, but he not being prefent, Signor Veroli beat time to the choruffes. Befides the verfes which Signor Manzoli fung in the mafs, with which I was very much delighted, though his voice feemed lefs powerful, even in a fmall church, than when he was in England; he performed a charming motet, compofed by Signor Monza, of Milan.

Signor Guarducci, and Signor Ricciarelli, left Florence a few days only before my arrival there, otherwife I might have heard a duo fung by Signor Man-

zoli

zoli and Signor Guarducci, who performed together at a private concert. this was a lofs the more to be regretted, as thefe two great performers are feldom in the fame place, and very rarely fing together.

At prefent, though Florence does not abound in mufical geniuffes of it's own growth, yet it is very well fupplied from other places, for, befides the performers above mentioned, Signor Campioni is fettled here, as *maeftro di Capella* to the grand duke, Signor Dottel, the celebrated performer on the German flute, is of his band, and Signor Nardini is engaged here, as principal violin, in the fervice of the fame prince *.

I heard likewife in this city a good performer on the double harp, Signora Anna Fond, from Vienna, who is in the fervice of the court, and my little countryman, Linley, who had been two years under

* Thefe three eminent mafters, whofe merit is well known to all Europe, have been lately tempted to quit Leghorn, by the munificence of the grand duke.

Signor

Signor Nardini, was at Florence when I arrived there, and was univerſally admired. The *Tommaſino*, as he is called, and the little Mozart, are talked of all over Italy, as the moſt promiſing geniuſſes of this age.

The comedy of *il Saggio Amico*, by Goldoni, which I had ſeen at Breſcia, was repreſented this evening at another theatre, larger and more ſplendid than that where I had ſeen the burlettas. I found ſo much company there, that it was impoſ-ſible to procure a ſeat · the play was dull, but there was a Turkiſh dance between the acts, which laſted near half an hour : it was very ingenious, and the ſcenes and dreſſes were the moſt magnificent I had ever ſeen in my life *.

In my way to this theatre, juſt as it was growing dark, I met in the ſtreets a company of *Laudiſti* : they had been at Fieſole, and were proceeding in proceſ-ſion to their own little church. I had

---

* The price for the pit in this theatre, and for that of every comic opera in Italy, is one paul, a-mounting to almoſt ſix pence Engliſh.

the

the curiosity to follow them, and procured a book of the words they were singing *. They stopt at every church in their way, to sing a stanza in three parts; and when they arrived at their own church, into which I gained admission, there was a band of instruments to receive them, who, between each stanza that they sung, played a symphony. They performed vespers in *Canto Fermo*, assisted by their chaplain: the whole was conducted with great decorum, and was certainly a very innocent amusement. Some of the companies of *Laudisti*, in Florence, have subsisted near five hundred years. I found a folio MS. of *Laudi Spirituali*, with the notes, in the Magliabecchi library, composed for the company of friars of the order of the *Umiliati*, and sung at the church of All Saints, Florence, 1336.

Monday, Sept 10. This afternoon, I
* The title of these hymns runs thus, *Laudi da Cartarsi da Fratelli della venerabil Compagnia di S M Maddalena de' pazzi e S Guiseppe in S Maria in Campidoglio in Firenze*, 1770.

had

had the pleafure of hearing Signor Nardini, and his little fcholar Linley, at a great concert, at the houfe of Mr. Hempfon, an Englifh gentleman, where there was much company. This gentleman plays the common flute in a particular manner, improving the tone very much, by inferting a piece of fpunge into the mouth-piece, through which the wind paffes. He performed two or three difficult concertos, by Haffe, and Nardini, very well. There was a perfon from Perugia, who played a folo on the viol d'amore, very agreeably; and Signor Nardini played both a folo and a concerto, of his own compofition, in fuch a manner as to leave nothing to wifh; his tone is even and fweet; not very loud, but clear and certain; he has a great deal of expreffion in his flow movements, which, it is faid, he has happily caught from his mafter Tartini. As to execution, he will fatisfy and pleafe more than furprize: in fhort, he feems the completeft player on

the

the violin in all Italy, and, according to my feelings and judgment, his stile is delicate, judicious, and highly finished [*].

The Tommasino Linley played two concertos, very much in the manner of his master. Signor Nardini has a great number of young professors under his care, as his master, Tartini, used to have, among whom is a son of Mr. Agus, from England.

Tuesday 11. At another great *accademia*, at the house of Signor Domenico Baldigiani, I this evening met with the famous *Improvvisatrice*, Signora Maddalena Morelli, commonly called *La Corilla*, who is likewise a scholar of Signor Nardini, on the violin; and afterwards I was frequently at her house [+]. Besides

[*] Whoever has heard the polished performance of the celebrated Madame Sirmen, may form a pretty just idea of Signor Nardini's manner of playing.

[+] She has, almost every evening, a *conversazione*, or assembly, which is much frequented by the foreigners, and men of letters, at Florence.

her

her wonderful talent of fpeaking verfes *extempore* upon any given ſubject, and being able to play a *ripieno* part, on the violin, in concert, fhe fings with a great deal of expreffion, and has a confiderable fhare of execution

I was feveral times at the houfe of Signor Campioni, whofe trios have been fo well received in England He is married to a lady who paints very well, and who is likewife a neat performer, on the harpfichord. He has the greateft collection of old mufic, particularly Madrigals, of the fixteenth and feventeenth centuries; Padre Martini's excepted, that I ever faw: he has likewife himfelf compofed a great deal for the church, fince his eftablifhment at Florence. He fhewed me the fcore of a *Te Deum*, which he fet for the birth of the grand duke's eldeft daughter, full of curious canons, and ingenious contrivances : it was performed by a band of two hundred voices and inftruments.

Among

Among the *Dilettanti*, at Florence, the Marquis of Ligniville is regarded as a good theorist and composer. He has set the hymn *Salve Regina* in *Canon*, for three voices. The music is neatly engraved, and copies of it are given to his friends. The Marquis was not in Florence during my residence there; however, I was presented with a copy of this curious piece, by a musician in the service of his excellence *.

Mr. Perkins, an English gentleman, who has resided a considerable time in this city and in Bologna, is likewise a good musician. A letter from Padre

* In the title page of this *Salve Regina*, the Marquis of Ligniville is stiled Prince of Conca, chamberlain to their Imperial Majesties, director of the music of the court in Tuscany, and member of the philharmonic society of Bologna. He is Prince of Conca, in the kingdom of Naples, by right of his mother, is son of the famous Marshal Ligniville, who was killed in the gardens of Colorno, a country house belonging to the Duke of Parma, during the war of 1733

Martini

Martini procured me the honour of his acquaintance. This gentlemen is entitled to my beft acknowledgments for many mufical curiofities, with which he was fo kind to furnifh me; and among the reft, for an effay, of which he is himfelf the author, on the capacity and extent of the violoncello, in imitating the violin, flute, French horn, trumpet, hautboy, and baffoon.

At Florence, I found the harpfichord of Zarlino, which is mentioned in the fecond part of his Harmonical Inftitutions, p 140. This inftrument was invented by Zarlino, in order to give the temperament and modulation of the three *genera*, the diatonic, chromatic, and enharmonic; and was conftructed, under his direction, in the year 1548, by Dominico Pefarefe: it is now in the poffeffion of Signora Moncini, widow of the late compofer Pifcetti. I copied Zarlino's inftructions for tuning it, from his own hand-writing, on the back of the fore-

board,

board.; but I shall reserve them, and the particular description of this curious instrument, for the History of Music, to which they more properly belong.

The grand duke's gallery, the Pitti palace, the Lorenziana, the Magliabecchi, and the Rinuccini libraries, all furnished reflections and materials for my intended work; and the conversations with which I was honoured by Dr. Bicchierai, Dr. Perelli, professor of mathematics, Dr. Guadagni, professor of experimental philosophy, il proposto Dr. Fossi, Signor Bandini, librarian to the grand duke, and others; who facilitated my enquiries, and afforded me every opportunity for information I could wish, rendered by residence, in this delightful city, to which all the arts have been so much and so long indebted, at once both pleasant and profitable.

S I E N N A.

There had been an opera, in this city, during the month of August, in which

Signor

Signor Nicolini was the principal finger,
and very much approved ; but fo capri-
cious is public favour, that, with the
fame talents, the fame voice, the fame
performers, and in the fame compofitions,
he was totally difliked and neglected, at
Lucca, in the month of September!

MONTEFIASCONE.

September 18. In my way to Rome, I
vifited Signor Guarducci, who has here
built himfelf a very good houfe, and fitted
it up in the Englifh manner, with great
tafte.   He had already been apprized of
my journey into Italy, and received me
in the politeft manner imaginable.   He
was fo obliging as to let me hear him, in
a fong of Signor Sacchini's compofition,
which he fung divinely.   His voice, I
think, is more powerful than when he
was in England, and his tafte and expreffion feem to have received every poffible degree of felection and refinement.
He is a very chafte performer, and adds
but

but few notes; thofe few notes, however,
are fo well chofen, that they produce
great effects, and leave the ear thoroughly
fatisfied. He has a winter-houfe in Florence, and has built this at Montefiafcone,
the place of his birth, to retire to in fummer, and to receive his mother, and his brothers and fifters : it is charmingly fituated,
commanding, on one fide, a fine profpect
of the country, as far as Aquapendente,
and a great part of the Lake of Bolfena;
and, on the other, the hills of Viterbo,
and the country leading to it. He fays
he has totally quitted the ftage, and intends finging no more in public : this is
a lofs to Italy, as I find he is now allowed by the Italians the firft place among
all the fingers of the prefent period; and,
at Rome, they ftill fpeak of his performance, in Piccini's *Didone Abbandonata*,
with rapture. Signor Guarducci, in a
manner truly obliging, gave me letters to
eminent profeffors at Rome and Naples,
and not only treated me with the greateft
hofpitality,

hofpitality while under his roof, but load-
ed my chaife with exquifite wine, the produce of his own vineyard, and with other
refrefhments *.

R O M E.

It is impoffible to approach this city,
the capital of the world, for fuch it *ftill
is* with refpect to the arts, without fen-
fations which no other fituation can excite. The remains of antiquity, like the
Sibyls works of old, become of greater
value the lefs there is of them. At a traveller's firft entrance into Rome, every
ftick, half devoured by time, or ftone in-
crufted with mofs, is fo interefting, that
his curiofity is not to be fatisfied but by
a moft minute examination of it; left
the precious fragments of fome venerable pile, or the memorial of fome illuf-
trious atchievement, fhould be paffed
unnoticed.

* The wine of Montefiafcone is proverbially famous all over Italy.

S   Though

Though my views and expectations, on arriving in this city, were chiefly confined to antiquities, and the inedited materials with which the Vatican and other libraries might furnish me, relative to *ancient music*, yet I received great pleasure from the *modern*.

September 21. The day after my arrival, at his Grace the Duke of Dorset's, I heard Signor Celestini, the principal violin here, who is a very neat, and expressive performer : he was seconded by Signor Corri, who is an ingenious composer, and sings in a very good taste ; there was likewise a good performer on the violoncello.

Signor Celestini played, among other things, one of his own solos, which was very pleasing, though extremely difficult, with great brilliancy, taste, and precision.

Saturday, *Sept.* 22. This evening Mr. Beckford, to whose zeal for the business in which I am embarked I have infinite obliga-

obligations, made a concert for me, consisting of twelve or fourteen of the best performers in Rome; these were led by Signor Celestini. There were three voices, Signor Cristofero, of the Pope's chapel, who sings very much in Guarducci's way, and is little inferior to him in delicacy; *il Graffetto*, a boy, who submitted to mutilation by his own choice, and against the advice of his friends, for the preservation of his voice, which is indeed a very good one, and he is, in other respects, a very pleasing singer; and a *buffo* tenor, a very comical fellow.

September 23. I was introduced to Signor Crispi, a celebrated *Maestro di Capella*, at whose house there was an *accademia* this evening, in which the vocal part was performed by his wife. This composer has an *accademia* at his house every Friday evening, at which there is usually a good band and much company.

Septem-

September 24. There was a grand *Fun-zioni* at the *Santi Apoftoli*, on account of the reconciliation of the Pope and the King of Portugal. It was at this church that I firft faw his Holinefs, and a great number of Cardinals, and heard *Te Deum*. There were two large bands of mufic, and an immenfe crowd. The mufic was compofed by Signor Mofi. Criftofero fung charmingly; the airs were pretty, but the choruffes poor.

In the evening the outfide of the cupola, church, and colonade of St. Peter, together with the Vatican palace, were finely illuminated, which affords a fpectacle to the inhabitants of Rome, not to be equalled in the univerfe. And in the balconies, next to the ftreet, at the palaces of moft of the Cardinals, befides illuminations, there were concerts of very numerous bands of inftrumental performers, but chiefly at the refidence of the Portuguefe Ambaffador, where the hands employed amounted to above a
hun-

hundred, and thefe continued their performance all night. However, this mufic, though in the open air, was too noify
for me, and I retreated from it early, in
order to have my ears foothed with more
placid founds at the Duke of Dorfet's
concert.

Tuefday 25. I had this morning the
honour of being prefented to Cardinal
Alexander Albani, principal librarian to
the Vatican, and *Prefetto*, or Governor
of the Pope's chapel. His eminence received me in the moft obliging and con-
defcending manner imaginable, taking me
by the hand, and faying, *Figlio mio, che
voleti?* " My fon, what do you wifh I
" fhould do for you?" And upon my
telling the views with which I came into
Italy, and expreffing a defire to be permitted to examine MSS. in the Vatican
library, and in the archives of the ponti-
fical chapel, relative to mufic, he faid,
" You fhall have the permiffion you de-
" fire, but write it down in the form of

" a

" a memorial," which being done, he
called for his secretary, to whom he gave
instructions to draw up an order, which
he signed, and addressed to *Monsignore
l'Arcivescovo di Apomea, prefetto della Va-
cana*, to admit me into the Vatican library when I pleased, to let me see what
books and MSS I pleased, and to have
copied what I pleased.

This was an important point gained,
but, without the intelligence and assistance of the Abate Elie, one of the *custodi*,
or keepers of the books in the Vatican,
I should have been but little the better
for the permission I had obtained. For
the MSS. in this celebrated library are so
numerous, and many of them in such
disorder, that to find the tracts I wished
would have been a work of years, had
he not pointed them out *. This gentleman employed five or six whole days

---

* As yet there is no regular catalogue of the
western MSS in the Vatican library One was
made and printed some years ago, in fourteen volumes

in making a catalogue for me of all that the Vatican contained relative to my work; after which I regularly fpent my mornings there, in reading and marking fuch things as I wifhed to have copied entirely, or from which I was defirous of extracts; and thefe my good friend the Abate undertook to tranfcribe for me, while I went to Naples.

During my firft refidence at Rome, I had fo much to fee, and fo many enquiries to make, relative to ancient mufic, and fpent fo much time in the Vatican and other libraries, that I had but little to fpare for the modern; however, that little was fpent much to my fatisfaction, in hearing public performances in the churches, and private concerts in the houfes of feveral profeffors, as well as perfons of diftinction. But as many days were fpent here in much the fame man-

lumes folio, of the eaftern, but the author died before he had completed the work, and it has never fince been refumed by any other.

ner,

ner, to avoid repetition, I fhall, for the prefent, drop the journal ftile, and try to recollect the principal mufical events which happened while I was at Rome, without attending to dates; and, in enumerating thefe I fhould think myfelf guilty of ingratitude, if I paffed over in filence the countenance and affiftance with which I was honoured by my own countrymen. I hope I fhall therefore be pardoned the liberty of naming them occafionally, with the refpect due to their rank, and the fervices I received from them.

And firft, I cannot refift the vanity of faying, that I paffed few nights at Rome without hearing mufic at the Duke of Dorfet's, and that his grace had the goodnefs to contrive to have my curiofity gratified by fomething new and curious, either in compofition or performance, at moft of thefe concerts. It was here that I had an opportunity of meeting the beft performers in Rome, at a time when the

theatres

theatres were shut, and it would have been difficult to have heard them elsewhere

To Mr. Leighton, whose performance and taste in music are superior to those of most gentlemen, I am indebted for some curious compositions, and for the conversation of several persons in Rome, eminent for their skill in the art, and learning in the science of found; among whom were the Marchese Gabriele, and Monsignor Reggio.

To the counsel and assistance of those eminent antiquaries, Messieurs Jenkins, Morrison, and Byers, I owe the greatest part of my original drawings of ancient instruments; and to their active friendship I likewise owe much of the pleasure and information I received at Rome.

And now, having acknowledged these debts to my countrymen, I must again say, that the men of learning and genius among the Italians have, throughout my journey, treated me with the utmost

hos-

hofpitality and kindnefs, each feeming to
ftrive who fhould moft contribute to my
information and amufement. For, except the civilities with which I was honoured at Venice and Florence by Mr.
Richie, Sir Horace Mann, and Meffieurs
Perkins and Hempfon, I owe all my information and entertainment, till my arrival at Rome, to the Italians themfelves.
Indeed, it was to them I chiefly addreffed myfelf, thinking it moft profitable, both in point of language and
information, to mix with the natives.
But at Rome and Naples I met with fo
many Englifh, and found them all fo
ready to countenance and affift me in my
enquiries, that I had no occafion, or,
indeed, time, to deliver feveral letters,
with which I was furnifhed, to eminent
perfons, in the literary and mufical world,
at thofe two capitals.

However, among the Romans I muft
diftinguifh *il Cavalier Pirenefe*, who gave
me feveral drawings, and pointed out

4 proper

proper objects for others, of such ancient instruments as still subsist entire, among the best remains of antiquity; the A-bate Orsini, a great collector of musical compositions and tracts, who, among other useful materials for my intended work, furnished me with a sight and catalogue of all the musical dramas that have been performed at Rome, from the beginning of the last century to the present time, Counsellor Reiffenstein, who, though not a native of Rome, has lived so long there, and is possessed of so much learning and taste in the fine arts, that I found myself much enlightened by his conversation, and indebted to his zeal and intelligence for very singular services; and the Cavalier Santarelli, *Ca-pellano di Malta* *, and *Maestro di Capella* to his Holiness.

To Signor Santarelli I was favoured with a letter from Padre Martini, which

* As Capellano di Malta he wears a small cross and an ivory star on his breast.

had

had all the effect I could wifh, as I foon found this excellent mufician and worthy man, not only difpofed to treat me with politenefs, but even with friendfhip in the utmoft extent of the word : he was the more able to render me real fervices in my mufical enquiries, as, befides his ftation in the Pope's chapel, and his great fkill and experience in the practical part, I found him deep in the theory, and learned in the hiftory of his profeffion, having been many years employed in the following curious work, *Della Mufica del Santuario e della difciplina de fuoi Cantori*; or, an Hiftorical Differtation on Church Mufic. This work is divided into different centuries fince the time of our Saviour, as *feccolo primo, fec fecundo, fec. terza*, &c. giving authorities throughout, from ecclefiaftical hiftory. The firft volume was printed in the year 1764, but has never yet been publifhed . the fecond, in MS. is in great forwardnefs ; it feems to fupply all the deficiencies of another

curious

curious and fcarce work on the fame fubject, publifhed in 1711, called *Offervazi-*
oni per ben regolare il coro della Capella pon-
tificia ; or, Rules for conducting the Choir
of the Pope's Chapel, by Andrea Adamo ;
but the hiftorical part of this book, beginning only at the year 1400, and end-
ing in 1711, that of Signor Santerelli,
which begins with the earlieft ages of
the church, and continues to the prefent
time, would certainly be a valuable
acquifition to fuch lovers of church
mufic as wifh to trace it from it's
fouice *.

* It feems as if Signor Santarelli was prevented
from publifhing his work, by the want of a patron
worthy of it   He is fo fenfible of the contempt
with which mufic is treated at prefent, by the
firft dignitaries of the church, that he entertains
but fmall hopes of the fuccefs of his book, though
it has been a work of much time and labour, and
feems worthy the patronage and protection of his
Holinefs, for the ufe of whofe fervants, as well as
for the fervice of mufic in general, it is in an
eminent degree calculated

Befides

Befides communicating to me his unpublifhed printed book, and the fecond
volume in MS. Signor Santarelli obliged
me with extracts from two MS. volumes
of curious anecdotes, and paffages from
old and fcarce books relative to mufic;
the whole collected in the courfe of many
years converfation and reading. I muft
add to thefe favours, that of procuring
me fome of the moft curious and fcarce
printed books which I fought at Rome:
it was owing to his friendly zeal likewife,
that, after three weeks fpent in vain by
myfelf and friends there, in fearch of the
firft *oratorio* that was ever fet to mufic, I
at length got a fight and copy of it; and,
to crown the whole, he joined to all thefe
benefits, not only that of furnifhing me
with a true and genuine copy of the famous *Miferere* of *Allegri*, but all the compofitions performed in the Pope's chapel
during Paffion Week; together with
many others of *Paleftrina, Benevoli, Lucca
Marenza,* and others which have never
been

been printed, nor have they ever been performed but in that chapel.

I was not more curious about the Vatican library, than the Pope's chapel, that celebrated fanctuary in which church mufic feems to have had it's birth, or at leaft to have received its firft refinement; and concerning this chapel I was favoured with all the fatisfaction I could wifh from the Cav. Santarelli.

In the Pope's, or Siftine chapel, no organ, or inftrument of any kind, is employed in accompanying the voices, which confift of thirty-two; eight bafes, eight tenors, eight counter-tenors, and eight fopranos, or trebles; thefe are all in ordinary: there is likewife a number of fupernumeraries ready to fupply the places of thofe who are occafionally abfent, fo that the fingers are never fewer than thirty-two, on common days, but on great feftivals they are nearly doubled *.

* Befides the fupernumerary *expectants* of this chapel, many of the capital opera fingers from

other

The dreſs of the ſingers in ordinary, is a kind of purple uniform; their pay is not great, and at preſent ſubjects of ſuperior merit, belonging to this eſtabliſhment, meet with but little notice or encouragement, ſo that muſic here begins to degenerate and decline very much, to which the high ſalaries given to fine voices and ſingers of great abilities in the numerous operas throughout Italy, and, indeed, all over Europe, greatly contribute, by little and little, all thoſe embelliſhments and refinements in the execution of ancient muſic, as well as the elegant ſimplicity for which that of this chapel is ſo celebrated, will be loſt. Formerly, even the *Canto Fermo* was here infinitely ſuperior to that of every other place by its purity, and by the expreſſive manner in which it was chanted.

I had indeed been told, before my arrival at Rome, by a friend who had re-

other parts of Italy, are employed in Paſſion Week.

ſided

fided there nineteen years, that I muſt not expect to find the muſic of the Pope's chapel ſo ſuperior in the performance to that of the reſt of Italy, as it had been in times paſt, before operas-were invented and ſuch great ſalaries given to the principal ſingers ; *then* the Pope's muſicians being better paid, were conſequently more likely to be poſſeſſed of abilities ſuperior to thoſe elſewhere, but, at preſent, this is not the caſe, and the conſequence is obvious; their ſituation is ſomewhat ſimilar to that of our choriſters and choirmen in England, where their ſalaries remain at the original eſtabliſhment, and at that point of perfection their performance ſeems to remain likewiſe ; living is dearer; money of leſs value ; more is given elſewhere; another profeſſion is uſually tacked to that of ſinging, in order to obtain a livelihood; and church muſic, of courſe, falls into decay, and goes from bad to worſe, while that of the theatres re-

T   ceives

ceives daily improvements by additional
rewards *.

* See remarks on Mr. Avifon's Eſſay on Muſical
Expreſſion, publiſhed 1753, in which the author has
well explained the cauſes of degeneracy in our
church muſic, and the want of ſkill in the performers
of it. With reſpect to theſe he ſays, " I believe
" if the ſtatutes of every cathedral were examined,
" it would appear, that the ſalary allotted to each
" member was exactly proportioned one to the other
" perhaps thus ; to the choriſter, or ſinging boy,
" five pounds ; to the ſinging man, ten ; to the
" minor canon, twenty ; the organiſt the ſame;
" to the canon or reſidentiary, forty , and to the
" dean, eighty pounds *per annum*, which, if mul-
" tiplied by four, would make the firſt twenty, the
" ſecond forty, the third eighty, the fourth one
" hundred and ſixty, and the fifth three hundred
" and twenty . this, with the chance of livings to
" the clergy, would be a decent competency for
" each in his ſtation , and I may venture to affirm,
" that the three former would be very well con-
" tented with it : yet, even this increaſe will not
" ſatisfy the two latter , but, without ſcruple or
" remorſe, they (by what authority I know not)
" divide three fourths of the profits ariſing from
" the portions allotted to their inferiors, among
" themſelves , a manifeſt abuſe of the founder's in-
" tention, and injuſtice to the ſeveral incumbents
" hence a canonry comes to be valued at two hun-
" dred,

Signor Santarelli favoured me with the following particulars relative to the famous *Miserere* of *Allegri* *. This piece, which, for upwards of a hundred and fifty years, has been annually performed in Passion Week at the Pope's chapel, on Wednesday and Good-Friday, and which, in appearance, is so simple as to make those, who have only seen it on paper, wonder whence its beauty and effect could arise, owes its reputation more to the manner in which it is performed, than to the composition: the same music is many times repeated to different words, and the singers have, by tradition, certain customs, expressions, and graces of convention, *(certe espressioni e Gruppi)* which produce

"dred, and a deanry at four hundred pounds *per annum*, and if this computation over-rates the value of some, others however must be allowed to exceed it greatly "

* *Miserere mei, Deus,* &c. Have mercy upon me, O God! ps. 51. *Gregorio Allegri* was a descendant of the famous painter Correggio, whose family-name was *Allegri.*

T 2   great

great effects; such as swelling and diminishing the sounds altogether; accelerating or retarding the measure at some particular words, and singing some entire verses quicker than others. Thus far Signor Santarelli. Let me add, from *Andrea Adami*, in the work mentioned above, that, " After several vain attempts by
" preceding composers, for more than a
" hundred years, to set the same words
" to the satisfaction of the heads of
" the church, Gregorio Allegri succeed-
" ed so well, as to merit eternal praise;
" for with few notes, well modulated,
" and well understood, he composed such
" a *Miserere* as will continue to be sung
" on the same days, every year, for ages
" yet to come; and one that is conceived
" in such just proportions as will asto-
" nish future times, and ravish, as at pre-
" sent, the soul of every hearer."

However, some of the great effects produced by this piece, may, perhaps, be justly attributed to the time, place, and solemnity

nity of the ceremonials, ufed during the performance: the pope and conclave are all proftrated on the ground; the candles of the chapel, and the torches of the baluf-trade, are extinguifhed, one by one; and the laft verfe of this pfalm is terminated by two choirs; the *Maeftro di Capella* beating time flower and flower, and the fingers diminifhing or rather *extinguifhing* the harmony, by little and little, to a per-fect point *.

It is likewife performed by felect voices, who have frequent rehearfals, particularly on the Monday in Paffion Week, which is wholly fpent in repeating and polifhing the performance.

This compofition ufed to be held fo facred, that it was imagined excommuni-cation would be the confequence of an attempt to tranfcribe it. Padre Martini

* Adami's inftructions are thefe ·——*Averta pure il Signor Maeftro che l'ultimo verfo del Salmo termina a due Cori, e però farà la Battuta Adagio, per finirlo Piano, fmorzando a poco, a poco l'Armonia.*

Offerv per reg il Coro della cap. pont p. 36.

told

told me there were never more than two
copies of it made by authority, one of
which was for the late king of Portugal,
and the other for himself: this laft he
permitted me to tranfcribe at Bologna,
and Signor Santarelli favoured me with
another copy from the archives of the
Pope's chapel: upon collating thefe two
copies, I find them to agree pretty exactly, except in the firft verfe. I have feen
feveral fpurious copies of this compofition
in the poffeffion of different perfons; in
which the melody of the *foprano*, or upper part, was tolerably correct, but the
other parts differed very much; and this
inclined me to fuppofe the upper part to
have been written from memory, which,
being fo often repeated to different words
in the performance, would not be difficult
to do, and the other parts to have been
made to it by fome modern contra-puntift
afterwards.

Before I quit a fubject fo interefting to
the lovers of church mufic, I fhall add
the

the following anecdote, which was given me likewife by Signor Santarelli.

The Emperor Leopold the firft, not only a lover and patron of mufic, but a good compofer himfelf, ordered his am- baffador, at Rome, to entreat the Pope to permit him to have a copy of the cele- brated *Miferere* of *Allegri*, for the ufe of the Imperial chapel at Vienna; which be- ing granted, a copy was made by the *Sig- nor Maeftro* of the Pope's chapel, and fent to the Emperor, who had then in his fervice fome of the firft fingers of the age; but, notwithftanding the abilities of the performers, this compofition was fo far from anfwering the expectations of the Emperor and his court, in the execu- tion, that he concluded the Pope's *Maeftro di Capella*, in order to keep it a myftery, had put a trick upon him, and fent him another compofition*. Upon which, in

* Signor Santarelli's words were thefe :——*Quan- tunque Cantato da Mufici foaviffimi, fece alla Corte di Vienna la Mifera Comparfa di un fempliciffimo falfo Bordone.*

T 4   great

great wrath, he fent an exprefs to his Holinefs, with a complaint againft the
Maeftro di Capella, which occafioned his
immediate difgrace, and difmiffion from
the fervice of the papal chapel; and in fo
great a degree was the Pope offended, at
the fuppofed impofition of his compofer,
that, for a long time, he would neither
fee him, or hear his defence; however,
at length, the poor man got one of the
cardinals to plead his caufe, and to acquaint his Holinefs, that the ftile of finging in his chapel, particularly in performing the *Miferere*, was fuch as could not
be expreffed by notes, nor taught or tranf-
mitted to any other place, but by example;
for which reafon the piece in queftion,
though faithfully tranfcribed, muft fail
in its effect, when performed elfewhere.
His Holinefs did not underftand mufic,
and could hardly comprehend how the
fame notes fhould found fo differently in
different places, however, he ordered
his *Maeftro di Capella* to write down his
defence,

defence, in order to be fent to Vienna, which was done; and the Emperor, feeing no other way of gratifying his wifhes with refpect to this compofition, begged of the Pope, that fome of the muficians in the fervice of his Holinefs, might be fent to Vienna, to inftruct thofe in the fervice of his chapel how to perform the *Miferere* of Allegri, in the fame expreffive manner as in the Siftine chapel at Rome, which was granted. But, before they arrived, a war broke out with the Turks, which called the emperor from Vienna; and the *Miferere* has never yet, perhaps, been truly performed, but in the Pope's chapel

I vifited feveral times, while I was at Rome, Signor Mazzanti, who not only fings with exquifite tafte, but is likewife an excellent mufician. He is both a reader and a writer on the fubject of mufic, as well as a confiderable collector of books and manufcripts. The richnefs

of

of his tafte, in finging, makes ample a-
mends for the want of force in his voice,
which is now but a thread. He has a
great collection of Paleftrini's compofitions, and furnifhed me with feveral of
them, which I could not get elfewhere.
Signor Mazzanti is famous for finging
the poem of Taffo to the fame melody as
the Barcarolles of Venice. This he does
with infinite tafte, accompanying himfelf
on the violin, with the harmony of which
he produces curious and pleafing effects.
I prevailed on him to write me down the
original melody, in order to compare it
with one that I took down at Venice,
while it was finging on the great canal. He
has compofed many things himfelf, fuch
as operas and motets for voices; and trios,
quartets, quintets, and other pieces for
violins. He plays pretty well on the
violin, and is in poffeffion of the moft
beautiful and perfect *Steiner* I ever faw.
He has advanced very far in the theory of
mufic;

mufic; has made, by way of ftudy, an abridgment of the modulation of Paleftrini, which is well felected and digefted; and he fhewed me a confiderable part of a mufical treatife, in manufcript, written by himfelf.

At Rome I alfo had frequent converfations with Rinaldo di Capua, an old and excellent Neapolitan compofer. He is the natural fon of a perfon of very high rank in that country, and at firft only ftudied mufic as an accomplifhment; but being left by his father with only a fmall fortune, which was foon diffipated, he was forced to make it his profeffion. He was but feventeen when he compofed his firft opera at Vienna. I have often received great pleafure from his compofitions; he is not in great fafhion at prefent, though he compofed an *intermezzo* for the *Capranica* theatre at Rome, laft winter, which had great fuccefs. He is very intelligent in converfation; but, though a

good-

good-natured man, his opinions are rather singular and severe upon his brother compofers. He thinks they have nothing left to do now, but to write themfelves and others over again ; and that the only chance they have left for obtaining the reputation of novelty and invention, arifes either from ignorance or want of memory in the public ; as every thing, both in melody and modulation, that is worth doing, has been often already done. He includes himfelf in the cenfure ; and frankly confeffes, that though he has written full as much as his neighbours, yet out of all his works, perhaps not above *one* new melody can be found, which has been wire-drawn in different keys, and different meafures, a thoufand times. And as to modulation, it muft be always the fame, to be natural and pleafing ; what has not been given to the public being only the refufe of thoufands, who have tried and rejected it,

either

either as impracticable or difpleafing: The only opportunity a compofer has for introducing new modulation in fongs, is in a fhort fecond part, in order to *fright* the hearer back to the firft, to which it ferves as a foil, by making it comparitively beautiful. He likewife cenfures with great feverity the noife and tumult of inftruments in modern fongs.

Signor Rinaldo di Capua has at Rome the reputation of being the inventor of accompanied recitatives; but in hunting for old compofitions in the archives of S. Gerolamo della Carità, I found an oratorio by Aleffandro Scarlatti, which was compofed in the latter end of the laft century, before Rinaldo di Capua was born, and in which are *accompanied recitatives*. But he does not himfelf pretend to the invention; all he claims is the being among the firft who introduced long *ritornellos*, or fymphonies, into the recitatives of ftrong paffion and diftrefs, which

which exprefs or imitate what it would
be ridiculous for the voice to attempt.
There are many fine fcenes of this kind
in his works, and Haffe, Galuppi, Jomelli, and Piccini have been very happy
in fuch interefting, and often fublime
compofitions.

In the courfe of a long life Rinaldo di
Capua has experienced various viciffitudes
of fortune, fometimes in vogue, fometimes neglected. However, when he
found old age coming on, he collected
together his principal works, fuch as had
been produced in the zenith of his fortune and fancy; thinking thefe would
be a refource in diftrefsful times. Thefe
times came; various misfortunes and
calamities befel him and his family,
when, behold, this refource, this fole refource, the accumulated produce of his
pen, had, by a gracelefs fon been fold
for wafte paper !

The

The Roman performers from whom I received the greatest pleasure, were, in the vocal, Signor Cristofero, of the Pope's chapel, for voice and high finishing; Signor Mazzanti for taste and knowledge of music; La Bacchelli, commonly called the *Mignatrice* *, for brilliancy and variety of stile; and the eldest daughter of the celebrated painter Cavalier Battoni, a *dilettante*, and scholar of Signor Santarelli, for art where no art appears, and for that elegant simplicity, and truly pathetic expression, which cannot be defined.

The best violin performers were, Signor Celestini, whom I before mentioned; Signor Niccolai, a worthy scholar of Tartini; and Signor Ruma, a young man whom I frequently heard at Signor Crispi's concerts, who plays with great facility and neatness.

* Her profession is not music, but painting in miniature.

The

The Abàte Rossi is reckoned the neat-
eft harpsichord player at Rome; and
Signor Crispi, without pretension, is a
good performer on that instrument. But,
to say the truth, I have neither met with
a *great* player on the harpsichord, nor an
original composer for it throughout Italy[*].
There is no accounting for this but by
the little use which is made of that instrument there, except to accompany the
voice. It is at present so much neglected
both by the maker and player, that it is
difficult to say whether the instruments
themselves, or the performers are the
worst [†].

---

[*] It seems as if Alberti was always to be pillag-
ed or imitated in every modern harpsichord lesson.

[†] To persons accustomed to English harpsichords, all the keyed instruments on the continent
appear to great disadvantage. Throughout Italy
they have generally little octave spinets to accompany singing, in private houses, sometimes in a tri-
angular form, but more frequently in the shape of
our old virginals , of which the keys are so noisy,
and the tone so feeble, that more wood is heard
than wire. The best Italian harpsichord I met with

for

But with regard to the organ, I have frequently heard it judiciously and fpiritedly played in Italy. At Milan, San Martini has a way peculiar to himfelf of touching that inftrument, which is truly mafterly and pleafing. The firft organifts of St. Marc's church at Venice, of the Duomo at Florence, and of St. John Lateran at Rome (of whom I fhall have occafion to fpeak hereafter) are very fuperiour in their performance to moft others I have heard on the continent. But, in general, the beft organifts in Italy are the monks and friars, many of whom I have heard play in the churches

for touch, was that of Signor Grimani at Venice; and for tone, that of Monfignor Reggio at Rome; but I found three Englifh harpfichords in the three principal cities of Italy, which are regarded by the Italians as fo many phenomena. One was made by Shudi, and is in the poffeffion of the Hon. Mrs. Hamilton at Naples. The other two, which are of Kirkman's make, belong to Mrs. Richie at Venice, and to the Hon. Mrs. Earl, who refided at Rome when I was there.

U
and

and chapels of their own convents, not only in a masterly, but a brilliant and modern manner, without forgetting the genius of the inftrument. And fome of the girls of the Venetian Confervatorios, as well as the nuns in different parts of Italy, play with rapidity and neatnefs in their feveral churches; but there is almoft always a want of force, of learning, and courage in female performances, occafioned, perhaps, by that feminine foftnefs, with which, in other fituations, we are fo enchanted.

Having heard the moft eminent performers; converfed with the principal theorifts and compofers, found many of the books, manufcripts, and antiquities I had fought; and explained my wants with regard to the reft, to feveral friends at Rome, who kindly promifed me their affiftance in fupplying them during my abfence; I fet off for Naples on Sunday evening, the fourteenth of October.

NAPLES.

NAPLES.

I entered this city, impreſſed with the higheſt ideas of the perfect ſtate in which I ſhould find practical muſic. It was at Naples only that I expected to have my ears gratified with every muſical luxury and refinement which Italy could afford. My viſits to other places were in the way of *buſineſs*, for the performance of a *taſk* I had aſſigned myſelf; but I came hither animated by the hope of pleaſure. And what lover of muſic could be in the place which had produced the two Scarlattis, Vinci, Leo, Pergoleſe, Porpora, Farinelli, Jomelli, Piccini, and innumerable others of the firſt eminence among compoſers and performers, both vocal and inſtrumental, without the moſt ſanguine expectations. How far theſe expectations were gratified, the Reader will find in the courſe of my narrative, which is conſtantly a faithful tranſcript of my feelings at the time I entered them in my journal,

imme-

immediately after hearing and feeing, with a mind not confcious of any prejudice or partiality.

I arrived here about five o'clock in the evening, on Tuefday, October 16, and at night went to the *Teatro de' Fiorentini*, to hear the comic opera of *Gelofia per Gelofia*, fet to mufic by Signor Piccini. This theatre is as fmall as Mr. Foote's in London, but higher, as there are five rows of boxes in it. Notwithftanding the court was at Portici, and a great number of families at their *Villeggiature*, or country-houfes, fo great is the repution of Signor Piccini, that every part of the houfe was crowded. Indeed this opera had nothing elfe but the merit and reputation of the compofer to fupport it, as both the drama and finging were bad. There was, however, a comic character performed by Signor Cafaccia, a man of infinite humour; the whole houfe was in a roar the inftant he appeared; and the pleafantry of this actor did not con-

fift

fift in buffoonery, nor was it local, which in Italy, and, indeed, elfewhere, is often the cafe; but was of that original and general fort as would excite laughter at all times and in all places.

The airs of this burletta are full of pretty paffages, and, in general, moft ingeniously accompanied: there was no dancing, fo that the acts, of which there were three, feemed rather long.

There are three Confervatorios in this city, for the education of *boys* who are intended for the profeffion of mufic, of the fame kind with thofe of Venice, for *girls*. As the fcholars in the Venetian Confervatorios have been juftly celebrated for their tafte and neatnefs of execution, fo thofe of Naples have long enjoyed the reputation of being the firft *contra-puntifts* or compofers in Europe.

Wednefday 17. This afternoon I went to hear a mufical performance at the church of the Francifcans, where the three Confervatorios were to furnifh

mufic

mufic and muficians for a great feftival
of eight fucceffive days, morning and
evening*. This is a large handfome
church, but too much ornamented. The
architecture feems to be good, but it is
fo be-gilt that it almoft blinded me to
look at it; and in the few interftitial
parts where there is no gold, tawdry
flowers are painted in abundance.

The band was numerous, confifting
of above a hundred voices and inftruments. They were placed in a long oc-
cafional gallery, totally covered with gold
and filver gilding; but though the band
feemed to be a very good one, and the
leader very careful and attentive, yet the
diftance of fome of the performers from the
others, rendered it almoft impoffible that
the-time fhould be always exactly kept.

* It is by this performance that the Confervatorios hold their charters; and, in confideration of
the boys playing gratis, they are exempted by the
King from all taxes upon wine and provifions,
which are paid by the other inhabitants of Naples.

The

The compofition was by Signor Gennaro Manni, and in many movements admirable; he attended himfelf to beat the time. The opening was in a rough ftile; after which this fpecies of overture was made an accompaniment to a chorus, which was well written. Several airs and a duet fucceeded, which pleafed me extremely; there were fancy and contrivance, light and fhade; and though the finging was not of the firft clafs, yet there was a counter-tenor and a bafe which I liked very much. The counter-tenor had one of the moft powerful voices I ever heard; he made his way through the whole band, in the loudeft and moft tumultuous parts of the choruffes. When he had an air to fing alone, his fhake was good, and his ftile plain, but his *portamento* was a little deficient, and rather favoured of what we call in England the cathedral manner of finging, through the throat. The air which was given to the bafe was as ingenuoufly written as any I ever heard, the

accom-

accompaniments were full, without destroying the melody of the voice-parts: instead of shortening or mutilating its passages, the instruments seemed to continue and finish them, giving the singer time for respiration. In a duet between two *sopranos*, the accompaniments were likewise admirable; as they were in a chorus which had many solo parts in it. After this the author did not seem to be so happy. There were some trifling, and some heavy movements; in the former of which there was no other novelty than that of throwing the accent upon the wrong note; for instance, upon the second instead of the first; or, in common time, upon the fourth instead of the third. This may have its merit in comic operas, where some humour is seconded by it, but surely such a poor expedient is beneath the dignity of church music, where a grave and majestic stile should be preserved, even in rapid movements. But the same rage for novelty, which

which has occafioned fuch fudden revo-
lutions in the mufic of Italy, gives birth,
fometimes, to ftrange *concetti*.

The national mufic here is fo fingular, as to be totally different, both in
melody and modulation, from all I have
heard elfewhere. This evening in the
ftreets there were two people finging
alternately; one of thefe Neapolitan
Canzoni was accompanied by a violin
and *calafcione**. The finging is noify
and vulgar, but the accompaniments are
admirable, and well performed. The
violin and calafcione parts were incef-
fantly at work during the fong, as well
as the ritornels. The modulation furprifed me very much : from the key of A
natural, to that of C and F, was not difficult or new; but from that of A, with
a fharp third, to E flat, was aftonifhing;

* The Calafcione is an inftrument very common at Naples, it is a fpecies of guitar, with
only two ftrings, which are tuned fifths to each
other.

and

and the more fo, as the return to the orginal key was always fo infenfibly managed, as neither to fhock the ear, nor to be eafily difcovered by what road or relations it was brought about.

Thurfday 18. I was very happy to find, upon my arrival at Naples, that though many perfons to whom I had letters, were in the country, yet Signor Jomelli and Signor Piccini were in town. Jomelli was preparing a ferious opera for the great theatre of S. Carlo, and Piccini had juft brought the burletta on the ftage which I have mentioned before.

This morning I vifited Signor Piccini, and had the pleafure of a long converfation with him. He feems to live in a reputable way, has a good houfe, and many fervants and attendants about him. He is not more than four or five and forty; looks well, has a very animated countenance, and is a polite and agreeable little man, though rather grave in his manner for a Neapolitan poffeffed of fo

much

much fire and genius. His family is
rather numerous; one of his fons is a
ftudent in the univerfity of Padua. After
reading a letter which Mr. Giardini was
fo obliging as to give me to him, he told
me he fhould be extremely glad if he could
be of any ufe either to me or my work.
My firft enquiries were concerning the
Neapolitan Confervatorios ; for he having
been brought up in one of them himfelf,
his information was likely to be authen-
tic and fatisfactory. In my firft vifit I
confined my queftions chiefly to the four
following fubjects :

1. The antiquity of thefe eftablifhments.

2. Their names.

3. The number of mafters and fcholars.

4. The time for admiffion, and for
quitting thefe fchools.

To my firft demand he anfwered, that
the Confervatorios were of ancient ftanding, as might be feen by the ruinous condition

dition of one of the buildings, which was ready to tumble down *.

To my second, that their names were *S. Onofrio*, *La Pietà*, and *Santa Maria di Loreto*.

To my third question he answered, that the number of scholars in the first Conservatorio is about ninety, in the second a hundred and twenty, and in the other, two hundred.

That each of them has two principal *Maestri di Capella*, the first of whom superintends and corrects the compositions of the students, the second the singing, and gives lessons. That there are assistant masters, who are called *Maestri Secolari*, one for the violin, one for the violoncello, one for the harpsichord, one for the hautbois, one for the French horn, and so for other instruments.

* I afterwards obtained, from good authority, the exact date of each of these foundations, their fixed and stated rules, amounting to thirty-one, and the orders given to the Rectors for regulating the conduct and studies of the boys, every month in the year

To

To my fourth enquiry he anſwered, that boys are admitted from eight or ten to twenty years of age; that when they are taken in young they are bound for eight years; but, when more advanced, their admiſſion is difficult, except they have made a conſiderable progreſs in the ſtudy and practice of muſic. That after boys have been in a Conſervatorio for ſome years, if no genius is diſcovered, they are diſmiſſed to make way for others. That ſome are taken in as penſioners, who pay for their teaching; and others, after having ſerved their time out, are retained to teach the reſt; but that in both theſe caſes they are allowed to go out of the Conſervatorio at pleaſure.

I enquired throughout Italy at what place boys were chiefly qualified for ſinging by caſtration, but could get no certain intelligence. I was told at Milan that it was at Venice; at Venice, that it was at Bologna; but at Bologna the fact was denied, and I was referred to

fence; from Florence to Rome, and from
Rome I was fent to Naples. The operation moft certainly is againft law in all
thefe places, as well as againft nature; and
all the Italians are fo much afhamed of it,
that in every province they transfer it to
fome other.

" Afk where's the North ? at York, 'tis on the
    Tweed,
" In Scotland, at the Orcades; and there,
" At Greenland, Zembla, or the Lord knows
    where."   *Pope's Eff on Man.*

However, with refpect to the Confervatorios at Naples, Mr Gemineau, the
Britifh conful, who has fo long refided
there, and who has made very particular
enquiries, affured me, and his account was
confirmed by Dr. Cirillo, an eminent and
learned Neapolitan phyfician, that this
practice is abfolutely forbiden in the Confervatorios, and that the young *Caftrati*
came from Leccia in Apuglia; but, before
the operation is performed, they are
brought to a Confervatorio to be tried
as to the probability of voice, and
          then

2

then are taken home by their parents for this barbarous purpose. It is, however, death by the laws to all thofe who perform the operation, and excommunication to every one concerned in it, unlefs it be done, as is often pretended, upon account of fome diforders which may be fuppofed to require it, and with the confent of the boy. And there are inftances of its being done even at the requeft of the boy himfelf, as was the cafe of the Graffetto at Rome. But as to thefe previous trials of the voice, it is my opinion that the cruel operation is but too frequently performed without trial, or at leaft without fufficient proofs of an improvable voice; otherwife fuch numbers could never be found in every great town throughout Italy, without any voice at all, or at leaft without one fufficient to compenfate fuch a lofs. Indeed all the *mufici** in the churches at

* The word *mufico*, in Italy, feems now wholly appropriated to a finger with a *foprano* or *contr' alto* voice, which has been preferved by art.

pre-

prefent are made up of the refufe of the opera houfes, and it is very rare to meet with a tolerable voice upon the eftablifhment in any church throughout Italy. The *virtuofi* who fing there occafionally, upon great feftivals only, are ufually ftrangers, and paid by the time.

I went again this afternoon to the Francifcan's church, where there was a larger band than the day before. The whole Confervatorio of the Pietà, confifting of a hundred and twenty boys, all dreffed in a blue uniform, attended. The *Sinfonia* was juft begun when I arrived; it was very brilliant, and well executed : then followed a pretty good chorus; after which, an air by a tenor voice, one by a *foprano*, one by a *contr' alto*, and another by a different tenor; but worfe finging I never heard before, in Italy; all was unfinifhed and *fcholar-like*; the clofes ftiff, ftudied, and ill executed, and nothing like a fhake could be muftered out of the whole band of fingers. The *foprano* forced

the

the high notes in a falfe direction, till they penetrated the brain of every hearer; and the bafe finger was as rough as a maftiff, whofe barking he feemed to imitate. A young man played a folo concerto on the baffoon, in the fame incorrect and unmafterly manner, which drove me out of the church before the vefpers were finifhed.

From hence I went directly to the comic opera, which, to-night, was at the *Teatro Nuovo*. This houfe is not only lefs than the *Fiorentini*, but is older and more dirty. The way to it, for carriages, is through ftreets very narrow, and extremely inconvenient. This burletta was called *Le Trame per Amore*, and fet by Signor Giovanni Paefiello, *Maeftro di Capella Napolitano*. The finging was but indifferent; there were nine characters in the piece, and yet not one good voice among them; however, the mufic pleafed me very much; it was full of fire and fancy, the ritornels abounding

X   in

in new paffages, and the vocal parts in
elegant and fimple melodies, fuch as
might be remembered and carried away,
after the firft hearing, or be performed
in private by a fmall band, or even without any other inftrument than a harpfichord *. The overture, of one movement
only, was quite comic, and contained a
perpetual fucceffion of pleafant paffages,
There was no dancing, which made it neceffary to fpin the acts out to rather a
tirefome length. The airs were much
applauded, though it was the fourteenth
reprefentation of the opera. The author
was engaged to compofe for Turin, at the

* This is feldom the cafe in modern opera fongs,
fo crowded is the fcore and the orcheftra. Indeed
Piccini is accufed of employing inftruments to
fuch excefs, that in Italy no copyift will tranfcribe
one of his operas without being paid a zechin more
than for one by any other compofer. But in burlettas he has generally bad voices to write for,
and is obliged to produce all his effects with inftruments ; and, indeed, this kind of drama
ufually abounds with brawls and *fquabbles*, which
it is neceffary to enforce with the orcheftra.

next

next carnival, for which place he fet out while I was at Naples. The performance began about a quarter before eight, and continued till paft eleven o'clock.

Friday 19. This evening I went a third time to St. Francefco's church, and heard the performance of the fcholars of another Confervatorio, Santa Mara di Loreto. They appeared all in a white uniform, with a black kind of fafh. The finging was a little better than the day before, but the inftruments were hardly fo good. The firft air, after a fpirited overture and chorus, was fung by an inoffenfive tenor; then another air by a foprano, not quite fo; after which, a third air by a bafe voice, the direct contrary of inoffenfive. Such a bawling Stentor, with a throat fo inflexible, fure never exifted before. The divifions were fo rough and fo ftrongly marked, that they became quite grotefque and ridiculous; if it had not been for the ferious effect which his performance had on the

X 2　　　　melan-

melancholy audience, no one could pof-
fibly have fuppofed it to be ferious. A
folo on the coarfeft double bafe that
was ever played upon, would have been
melifluous, by comparifon. After him,
a middling counter-tenor fung, which
even fo ftrong a foil could not make a-
greeable; and then another foprano, not
at all a hopelefs fubject: his voice was
well toned, and he had a little improvable fhake. In fhort, this was the
only promifing finger I had heard for two
days. But to the bad voices, fo flovenly,
ignorant, and unfinifhed a manner was
added, that the people were fung out of
church as faft as they came in. There
was a young man who played folo parts
in the ritornels with a kind of clarinet,
which they call at Naples a *vox humana*;
another on the trumpet, and a third on the
hautbois; but in an incorrect and unin-
terefting manner. The boys who fung
had very poor cadences to their fongs,
which,

which, as they ufually had fecond parts, were always repeated after the *da capo*.

Saturday, 20. This morning I heard, at the fame church, the boys of the Con-feryatorio of *St. Onofrio*, who wear a white uniform. The performance was much the fame as that of the other two. Thefe feminaries, which have heretofore produced fuch great profeffors, feem at prefent to be but low in genius. However, fince thefe inftitutions, as well as others, are fubject to fluctuations, after being languid for fome time, like their neigh-bour Mount Vefuvius, they will, perhaps, blaze out again with new vigour.

Sunday 21, and *Monday* 22. were fpent in vifiting the environs of Naples. However, I arrived in town foon enough on Monday night to hear Paefiello's opera, a fecond time, at the *Teatro Nuovo*. It pleafed me full as much now as before, and in the fame places. The overture ftill feemed comic and original, the airs far from common, though in

general

general plain and fimple. If this 'compofer has any fault, it is in repeating paffages too often, even to five or fix times,
which is like driving a nail into a plaif-
tered wall; two or three ftrokes fix it
better than more, for after that number,
it either grows loofe, or recoils: thus an
energy is often given by reiterated ftrokes
on the tympanum, but too often repeated, they not only ceafe to make any
further impreffion, but feem to obliterate
thofe already made. I ftill think this
opera too long for want of the *intermezzi*
of dancing *.

Tuefday 23. This evening hearing in
the ftreet fome genuine Neapolitan finging, accompanied by a calafcioncina, a
mandoline, and a violin; I fent for the
whole band up ftairs, but, like other
ftreet mufic, it was beft at a diftance; in
the room it was coarfe, out of tune, and
out of harmony, whereas, in the ftreet,

* I was afterwards informed that dancing is not
allowed in any other theatre at Naples than that
of St Çarlo, which is the theatre royal.

I   it

it seemed the contrary of all this: however, let it be heard where it will, the
modulation and accompaniment are very
extraordinary.

In the canzone of to-night they began
in A natural, and, without well knowing
how, they got into the moſt extraneous
keys it is poſſible to imagine, yet without offending the ear. After the inſtruments have played a long ſymphony in
A, the finger begins in F, and-ſtops in
C, which is not uncommon or difficult;
but, after another ritornel, from F, he
gets into E flat, then cloſes in A natural;
after this there were tranſitions even into
B flat, and D flat, without given offence,
returning, or rather *ſliding*; always into
the original key of A natural, the inſtruments moving the whole time in quick
notes, without the leaſt intermiſſion.
The voice part is very ſlow, a kind of
pſalmody; the words, of which there
are many ſtanzas to the ſame air, are
in the Neapolitan language, which is as

dif-

different from good Italian, as Welfh
from Englifh. It is a very fingular fpecies of mufic, as wild in modulation, and
as different from that of all the reft of
Europe as the Scots, and is, perhaps, as
ancient, being among the common people merely traditional. However, the violin
player wrote down the melody of the
voice part for me, and afterwards brought
me fomething like the accompaniment;
but thefe parts have a ftrange appearance
when feen on paper together. I heard
thefe muficians play a great number of
Neapolitan airs, but all were different
from other mufic.

A little before Chriftmas, muficians
of this fort come from Calabria to Naples, and *their* mufic is wholly different
from this: they ufually fing with a
guitar and violin, not on the fhoulder,
but hanging down. Paefiello had introduced fome of this mufic into his comic
opera, which was now in run. Signor
Piccinni promifed to procure me fome of
thefe

these wild national melodies. Another
fort is peculiar to Apuglia, with which
the people are fet a-dancing and fweat-
ing; who either have, or would be
thought to have been bitten by the tarantula. Of this mufic Dr. Cirillo procured me a fpecimen. Signor Serrao, in
a differtation on the fubject, and Dr. Cirillo, who has made feveral experiments,
in order to determine the fact, are both
of opinion that the whole is an impofition, practifed by the people of Apuglia,
to gain money: that not only the cure
but the malady itfelf is a fraud. Dr. Cirillo affured me that he had never been
able to provoke the tarantula either to bite
himfelf or others upon whom he had re-
peatedly tried the experiment * However, the whole is fo throughly believed
by fome inocent people in the country,

* This account may perhaps diminifh the honour
of mufic, by augmenting the number of fceptics,
as to its *miraculous powers*; yet truth requires it
fhould be given.

that

that, when really bitten by other infects or animals that are poifonous, they take this method of dancing, to a particular tune, till they fweat, which, together with their faith, fometimes makes them whole. They will continue the dance, in a kind of frenzy, for many hours, even till they drop down with fatigue and laffi-tude.

Wednefday 24. I went again this even-ing to Piccini's opera, but was too late for the overture; the houfe was very full, and the mufic pleafed me more than the firft time. The airs are not fo familiar as thofe in Paefiello s opera, yet there is much better writing in them, and there are fome accompanied recitatives, in the ritornels of which, though feveral different parts are going on at the fame time, there is a clearnefs, and, if it may be fo called, a *tranfparency,* which is wondeful. The finging, as I before obferved, is wretch-ed; but there is fo much *vis comica* in Cafaccia, that his finging is never

thought

thought of; yet, for want of dancing, the acts are neceſſarily ſo long, that it is wholly impoſſible to keep up the attention; ſo that thoſe who are not talking, or playing at cards, uſually fall aſleep.

Thurſday 25. After dinner I went once more to hear the boys of St. Onofrio, at the Franciſcans church. They performed a Litany, that was compoſed by Durante *; the reſt of the muſic, which ſeemed to be that of a raw and inexperienced compoſer, was by a young man, who beat time. There was again a ſolo on the inſtrument called *la Voce Hu-*

---

* Durante, who has been dead ſome years, was a long time Maſter to the Conſervatorio of St Onofrio. From the character Mr. Rouſſeau has given of this compoſer, I had conceived the higheſt ideas of his merit, and in the courſe of my journey through Italy, I collected a great number of his compoſitions for the church. M. Rouſſeau's words in ſpeaking of him are very ſtrong. " *Durante eſt le plus grand harmoniſte de l'Italie, c'eſt à dire du monde.*" Dict. de Muſique.

mana;

mana; it is of an agreeable tone, has a great compass, but was not well played on. A concerto on the violin was likewise introduced, where hand and fire were difcovered by the player, but no tafte or finifhing.

Friday 26. This morning I firft had the pleafure of feeing and converfing with Signor Jomelli, who arrived at Naples from the country but the night before. He is extremely corpulent, and, in the face, not unlike what I remember Handel to have been, yet far more polite and foft in his manner. I found him in his night-gown, at an inftrument, writing. He received me very politely, and made many apologies for not having called on me, in confequence of a card I had left at his houfe; but apologies were indeed unneceffary, as he was butjuft come to town, and at the point of bringing out a new opera. that muft have occupied both his time and thoughts fufficiently. He had heard of me from Mr. Hamilton. I gave him

him Padre Martini's letter, and after he
had read it we went to business directly. I
told him my errand to Italy, and shewed
him my plan, for I knew his time was
precious. He read it with great attention, and conversed very openly and ra-
tionally; said the part I had undertaken was much neglected at present in
Italy; that the Conservatorios, of which,
I told him, I wished for information, were
now at a low ebb, though formerly so
fruitful in great men. He mentioned to
me a person of great learning, who had
been translating David's Psalms into excellent Italian verse, in the course of which
work, he had found it necessary to write
a differtation on the music of the ancients,
which he had communicated to him. He
said this writer was a fine and subtle
critic; had differed in several points from
Padre Martini, had been in correspon-
dence with Metastasio, and had received
a long letter from him on the subject of
lyric poetry and music; all which he
thought

thought neceffary for me to fee. He
promifed to procure me the book, and, to
make me acquainted with the author.
He fpoke very much in praife of Aleffandro
Scarlatti, as to his church mufic, fuch
as motets, maffes, and oratorios ; promifed to procure me information, concerning
the Confervatorios, and whatever elfe
was to my purpofe, and in his power.
He took down my direction, and affured
me that the inftant he had got his opera
on the ftage, he fhould be entirely at my
fervice. Upon my telling him that my
time for remaining at Naples was very
fhort, that I fhould even then have been
on the road in my way home, but for
his opera, which I fo much wifhed to
hear; that befides urgent bufinefs in
England, there was great probability of
a war, which would keep me a prifoner
on the continent : he, in anfwer to that,
and with great appearance of fincerity,
faid, if after I returned to England, any
thing of importance to my plan occured,

he

he would not fail of sending it to me. In short, I went away in high good humour with this truly great composer, who is indisputably one of the first of his profession now alive in the universe, for were I to name the living composers of Italy for the stage, according to my idea of their merit, it would be in the following order: Jomelli, Galuppi, Piccini, and Sacchini. It is, however, difficult to decide which of the two composers first-mentioned, has merited most from the public; Jomelli's works are full of great and noble ideas, treated with taste and learning; Galuppi's abound in fancy, fire, and feeling; Piccini has far surpassed all his cotemporaries in the comic stile; and Sacchini seems the most promising composer in the serious.

The Honourable Mr. Hamilton, the British minister at this court, whose taste and zeal for the arts, and whose patronage of artists, are well known throughout Europe, being out of town when I came

to

to Naples, did me the honour, as foon as he heard of my arrival, to invite me to his country-houfe, called *Villa Angelica,* at the foot of Mount Vefuvius ; and this day, after vifiting Signor Jomelli, I waited upon him for the firft time, and was received by him and his lady, not only with politenefs, but even kindnefs. I had the happinefs of continuing there with them two or three days, during which time, among other amufements, mufic was not wanting, as Mr. Hamilton has two pages of his houfhold, who are excellent performers, one on the violin, and the other on the violoncello.

Saturday 27. This evening, though I had a violent head-ach, yet, in order firft to brave, and then to footh the pain, I determined to try the medicinal power of mufic at Piccini's opera, and found, that though it did not cure, it alleviated the pain, and diverted my attention from it. The houfe was very full, and the actors were in great fpirits. I went

early

early enough, for the firſt time, to hear the overture; it is very pretty and fanciful, conſiſting of only two movements, in which the violins were confined to hard labour. With what pleaſed me before, I was more pleaſed now, it is impoſſible not to be delighted with the originality, and ſurpriſed at the reſources of this author.

Monday 29. Mr. Hamilton being returned to Naples, in order to gratify my muſical curioſity, made a great concert at his houſe, where there was much company, and where I had the ſatisfaction of meeting with the chief muſical performers of this city, among whom were the celebrated player on the violin Signor Barbella, and Orgitano, one of the beſt harpſichord players and writers for that inſtrument at Naples. But Mrs. Hamilton is herſelf a much better performer on that inſtrument than either he or any one I heard there. She has great neatneſs, and more expreſſion and meaning in her

Y   play-

playing, than is often found among lady-players; for ladies, it muſt be owned, though frequently neat in execution, ſeldom aim at expreſſion. Barbella rather diſappointed me, his performance has nothing very ſurpriſing in it now: he is not young, indeed; and ſolo playing is never wanted or regarded here; ſo that teaching and orcheſtra playing are his chief employments He performed, however, moſt admirably the famous Neapolitan air, which the common people conſtantly play at Chriſtmas to the Virgin, this he plays with a drone kind of bag-pipe baſe, in a very humorous, though delicate manner. But as a ſolo-player, though his tone is very even and ſweet, he is inferior to Nardini; and, indeed, to ſeveral others in Italy; but he ſeems to know muſic well, and to have a good deal of fancy in his compoſitions, with a tincture of not diſagreeable madneſs.

It was here that I had firſt the honour of being preſented to Lord Fortroſe, from whom I afterwards received many ſingular favours. I was likewiſe introduced to the French Conſul, M. D'Aſtier, who is a real connoiſſeur in muſic; perfectly well acquainted with the different ſtiles of all the great compoſers of Europe, paſt and preſent, and diſcriminates very well in ſpeaking of their ſeveral merits. To him I communicated my plan, and with him I had a very ſatisfactory converſation. In order, I believe, that I might have more time for muſical diſquiſitions with this gentleman, and Signor Barbella, there was a ſupper party ſelected of about ten or twelve, and we ſtaid till near two o'clock in the morning.

Barbella is the beſt natured creature imaginable, his temper, as one of the company obſerved, is as ſoft as the tone of his violin. By ſitting next to him, I acquired much biographical knowledge concerning old Neapolitan muſicians.

Mr.

Mr. Hamilton had offered to write to all
the governors of the feveral Confervatorios, but Signor Barbella very obligingly
undertook to get me all the information
I could defire of thefe celebrated mufical
fchools. And Lord Fortrofe, whom he
attends every morning, invited me to
meet him at his lordfhip's houfe, whenever I pleafed. So that from Barbella,
and a young Englifhman, Mr. Oliver, who
has been four years in the Confervatorio
of St. Onofrio, I obtained a fatisfactory
account of whatever was neceffary for
me to know concerning this part of my
bufinefs at Naples. Mr. Hamilton entered fo far into my views, as to take a
lift of my wants, in order to confider of
the beft method of getting them fupplied.

Wednefday, October 31. This morning
I went with young Oliver to his Confervatorio of St. Onofrio, and vifited all the
rooms where the boys practife, fleep, and
eat. On the firft flight of ftairs was a
trum-

trumpeter, screaming upon his instrument till he was ready to burst; on the second was a French horn, bellowing in the same manner. In the common practising room there was a *Dutch concert,* consisting of seven or eight harpsichords, more than as many violins, and several voices, all performing different things, and in different keys: other boys were writing in the same room; but it being holiday time, many were absent who usually study and practise in this room. The jumbling them all together in this manner may be convenient for the house, and may teach the boys to attend to their own parts with firmness, whatever else may be going forward at the same time; it may likewise give them force, by obliging them to play loud in order to hear themselves; but in the midst of such jargon, and continued dissonance, it is wholly impossible to give any kind of polish or finishing to their performance; hence the slovenly

coarsecoarfenefs fo remarkable in their public exhibitions; and the total want of tafte, neatnefs, and expreffion in all thefe young muficians, till they have acquired them elfewhere.

The beds, which are in the fame room, ferve for feats to the harpfichords and other inftruments. Out of thirty or forty boys who were practifing, I could difcover but two that were playing the fame piece: fome of thofe who were practifing on the violin feemed to have a great deal of hand. The violoncellos practife in another room; and the flutes, hautbois, and other wind inftruments, in a third, except the trumpets and horns, which are obliged to fag, either on the ftairs, or on the top of the houfe.

There are in this college fixteen young *caftrati*, and thefe lye up ftairs, by them-felves, in warmer apartments than the other boys, for fear of colds, which might not only render their delicate voices unfit

unfit for exercife at prefent, but hazard the entire lofs of them for ever.

The only vacation in thefe fchools, in the whole year, is in autumn, and that for a few days only: during the winter, the boys rife two hours before it is light, from which time they continue their exercife, an hour and a half at dinner excepted, till eight o'clock at night; and this conftant perfeverance, for a number of years, with genius and good teaching, muft produce great muficians.

After dinner I went to the theatre of St. Carlo, to hear Jomelli's new opera rehearfed. There were only two acts finifhed, but thefe pleafed me much, except the overture, which was fhort, and rather difappointed me, as I expected more would have been made of the firft movement; but as to the fongs and accompanied recitatives, there was merit of fome kind or other in them all, as I hardly remember one that was fo indifferent as not to feize the attention. The

Y 4

fubject

subject of the opera was Demofoonte; the names of the singers I knew not then, except Aprile, the first man, and Bianchi, the first woman. Aprile has rather a weak and uneven voice, but is constantly steady, as to intonation. He has a good person, a good shake, and much taste and expression. La Bianchi has a sweet and elegant toned voice, always perfectly in tune, with an admirable portamento; I never heard any one sing with more ease, or in a manner so totally free from affectation. The rest of the vocal performers were all above mediocrity; a tenor with both voice and judgment sufficient to engage attention; a very fine contr'alto; a young man with a soprano voice, whose singing was full of feeling and expression; and a second woman, whose performance was far from despicable. Such performers as these were necessary for the music, which is in a difficult stile; more full of instrumental effects than vocal. Sometimes it may be thought rather laboured,

but

but it is admirable in the *tout ensemble*; masterly in modulation, and in melody full of new passages *. This was the first rehearsal, and the instruments were rough and unsteady, not being as yet certain of the exact time or expression of the movements; but, as far as I was then able to judge, the composition was perfectly suited to the talents of the performers, who, though all good, yet not being of the very first and most exquisite class, were more in want of the assistance of instruments to mark the images, and enforce the passion, which the poetry points out.

The public expectation from this production of Jomelli, if a judgment may be formed from the number of persons who attended this first rehearsal, was very great; for the pit was crowded, and many of the boxes were filled with the families of persons of condition.

* Jomelli is now said to write more for the *learned few*, than for the *feeling many*.

The

The theatre of S. Carlo is a noble and elegant ſtructure: the form is oval, or rather the ſection of an egg, the end next the ſtage being cut. There are ſeven ranges of boxes, ſufficient in ſize to contain ten or twelve perſons in each, who ſit in chairs, in the ſame manner as in a private houſe. In every range there are thirty boxes, except the three loweſt ranges, which, by the king's box being taken out of them, are reduced to twenty-nine. In the pit there are fourteen or fifteen rows of ſeats, which are very roomy and commodious, with leather cuſhions and ſtuffed backs, each ſeparated from the other by a broad reſt for the elbow: in the middle of the pit there are thirty of theſe ſeats in a row.

November 1, being All Saints day, I went, at leaſt two miles, to the church of the Incurabili, where I was told there would be good muſic; but I found it miſerable. From hence I went to ſeveral others,

others, where I only heard bad music ill
performed.

Friday, Nov. 3. This day I visited his
Neapolitan majesty's museum, at Portici,
where I had enquiries to make concerning ancient instruments and MSS. which
were of real importance to my history.
In the third apartment of this curious
repository, where the ancient instruments
of surgery are placed, I met with the following musical instruments; three *Sys-
trums*, two with four brass bars, and one
with three; several *Crotoli* or cymbals;
Tambours de basque; a *Syringa*, with seven pipes; and a great number of broken
bone or ivory *tibiæ*.

But the must extraordinary of all these
instruments is a species of trumpets, found
in Pompeia not a year ago; it is a good
deal broken, but not so much so as to
render it difficult to conceive the entire
form.   There are still the remains of seven small bone or ivory pipes, which are
inserted in as many of brass, all of the
same

same length and diameter, which surround the great tube, and seem to terminate in one mouth-piece. Several of the small brazen pipes are broken, by which the ivory ones are laid bare, but it is natural to suppose that they were all blown at once, and that the small pipes were unisons to each other, and octaves to the great one. It used to be flung on the shoulder by a chain, which chain is preserved, and the place where it used to be fastened to the trumpet, is still visible. No such instrument as this has been found before, either in ancient painting or sculpture, which makes me the more minute in speaking of it. This singular species of trumpet was found in the *Corps de Garde*, and seems to be the true military *Clangor Tubarum*.

As no person is suffered to use a pencil in the museum, when the company with which I had seen it was arrived at the inn where we dined, Mr. Robertson, an ingenious young artist of the party, was so obliging

obliging as to make a drawing of it, from memory, in my tablets ; which all the company, confifting of feven, agreed was very exact.

In the ninth or tenth room are all the volumes as yet found in Herculaneum, of which only four have been rendered intelligible, thefe are Greek. One upon the Epicurean philofophy, one upon rhetoric, one upon morality, and one upon mufic ; each volume appears to be only a black cinder. I faw two pages, opened and framed, of the MS. upon mufic, written by Philodemus ; but it is not a poem on mufic, as Mr. de la Lande fays, nor a fatire againft it, as others fay ; but a confutation of the fyftem of Ariftoxenus, who, being a practical mufician, preferred the judgment of the ear to the Pythagorean numbers, or the arithmetical proportions of mere theorifts. Ptolemy did the fame afterwards. I converfed with Padre Antonio Pioggi about this MS. it was he who opened and explained it, and

he

he is now superintending, at a foundery,
the casting of a new set of Greek characters exactly, resembling those in which
it was written, and in which it is to
be published.

Every lover of learning laments the slow
manner in which they proceed in opening
these volumes. All that have been found
hitherto were in Herculaneum. Those
of Pompeia are supposed to have been
wholly destroyed by fire.

Saturday 3. At night I went to a little
neat new play-house, just opened; there
was a comedy in prose, a Turkish story,
ill told, and not well acted.

Sunday 4. I went this morning to S.
Gennaro, to hear the organ and to see the
chapel, and the pictures in it, by Dominichini; after which I was conducted to the
house of Don Carlo Cotumacci, master to the
Conservatorio of St. Onofrio, whom I heard
play on the harpsichord; and who gave me
a great number of anecdotes concerning the
music of old times. He was scholar to the

2   Cavalier

Cavalier Scarlatti, in the year 1719; and shewed me the lessons he received from that great master, in his own hand writing. He also gave me a very particular account of Scarlatti and his family. Signor Cotumacci, was Durante's successor. He plays, in the old organ stile, very full and learnedly, as to modulation; and has composed a great deal of church music, of which he was so obliging as to give me a copy of two or three curious pieces. He has had great experience in teaching; and shewed me two books of his own writing, in manuscript, one upon accompaniment, and one upon counterpoint. I take him to be more than seventy years of age.

At night I went to the first public representation of Signor Jomelli's opera of *Demofoonte*, in the grand theatre of *San Carlo*, where I was honoured with a place in Mr. Hamilton's box. It is not easy to imagine or describe the grandeur and magnificence of this spectacle. It being the great festival of St Charles and the

King

King of Spain's name-day, the court was in grand gala, and the houfe was not only doubly illuminated, but amazingly crowded with well-dreffed company*. In the front of each box there is a mirrour, three or four feet long, by two or three wide, before which are two large wax tapers; thefe, by reflection, being multiplied, and added to the lights of the ftage and to thofe within the boxes, make the fplendor too much for the aching fight. The King and Queen were prefent. Their Majefties have a large box in the front of the houfe, which contains in height and breadth the fpace of four other boxes. The ftage is of an immenfe fize, and the fcenes, dreffes, and decorations were extremely magnificent; and I think this theatre fuperior, in thefe particulars, as well as in the mufic, to that of the great French opera at Paris.

* The fourth of November is likewife celebrated as the name-day of the Queen of Naples and the Prince of Afturias.

I   The

"But M.˙ de la Lande, after allowing that
"the opera in Italy is very well" as to
music and words," concludes with saying
"that it is not, in his opinion, quite so in
other respects, and for the following reasons;

"1. There is scarce any machinery in
the operas of Italy *.

"2. There is not such a multitude of
rich and superb dresses as at Paris.

"3. The number and variety of the
actors are less †.

"4. The chorusses are fewer and less
laboured. And

"5. The union of song and dance is
neglected" ‡.

To all which objections, a real lover of
music would perhaps say, *so much the better.*

M. de la Lande, however, allows
that the hands employed in the orchestra

---

* The Italians have long given up those puerile
representations of flying gods and goddesses, of
which the French are still so fond and so vain.

† If the characters are fewer, the dresses must be
so, of course

‡ *Voyage d'un François,* Tom. vi

are

are more numerous and various, but complains that the fine voices in an Italian opera are not only too few, but are too much occupied by the mufic and its embellifhments to attend to declamation and gefture.

With regard to this laft charge, it is by no means a juft one; for whoever rememoers Pertici and Lafchi, in the burlettas of London, about twenty years ago, or has feen the Buona Figliuola there lately, when Signora Guadagni, Signor Lovatini, and Signor Morigi were in it, or in the ferious operas of paft times remembers Monticelli, Elifi, Mingotti, Colomba Mattei, Manfoli, or, above all, in the prefent operas has feen Signor Guadagni, muft allow that many of the Italians, not only recite well, but are *excellent actors*.

Give to a lover of mufic an opera in a noble theatre, at leaft twice as large as that of the French capital, in which the poetry and mufic are good, and the vocal

and

and inftrumental parts well, performed, and he will deny himfelf the reft without murmuring; though his ear fhould be lefs ftunned with choruffes, and his eye lefs dazzled with machinery, dreffes, and dances than at Paris.

But to return to the theatre of S. Carlo, which, as a fpectacle, furpaffes all that poetry or romance have painted: yet with all this, it muft be owned that the magnitude of the building, and noife of the audience are fuch, that neither the voices or inftruments can be heard diftinctly. I was told, however, that on account of the King and Queen being prefent, the people were much lefs noify than on common nights. There was not a hand moved by way of applaufe during the whole reprefentation, though the audience in general feemed pleafed with the mufic : but, to fay the truth, it did not afford me the fame delight as at the rehearfal ; nor did the fingers, though they exerted themfelves more, appear

to

to equal advantage : not one of the prefent voices is fufficiently powerful for
fuch a theatre, when fo crowded and fo
noify. Signora Bianchi, the firft woman, whofe fweet voice and fimple manner of finging gave me and others fo
much pleafure at the rehearfal, did not
fatisfy the Neapolitans, who have been
accuftomed to the force and brilliancy of
a Gabrieli, a Taiber, and a de Amici,
There is too much fimplicity in her
manner for the depraved appetites of thefe
erfans gates, who are never pleafed but
when aftonifhed. As to the mufic, much
of the *claire obfcure* was loft, and nothing
could be heard diftinctly but thofe noify
and furious parts which were meant
merely to give relief to the reft; the mez-
zotints and back-ground were generally
loft, and indeed little was left but the
bold and coarfe ftrokes of the compofer's
pencil

During the performance, Caffarelli
came into the pit, and Signor Giraldi,
who

who was in Mr. Hamilton's box, propofed to make us acquainted; and at
the end of the performance, he conducted me to him; he looks well, and has a
very lively and animated countenance;
he does not feem to be above fifty years
of age, though he is faid to be fixty-
three. He was very polite, and entered
into conversation with great eafe and
chearfulnefs; he enquired after the
Dutchefs of Manchefter, and Lady Fanny
Shirley, who had honoured him with
their protection when he was in England,
which, he faid, was in the end of Mr.
Heydegger's reign. He introduced me
to Signor Gennaro Manno, a celebrated
Neapolitan compofer, who fat behind
him. Signor Giraldi had been with him
before, to fix a time for bringing me to
his houfe, it was now fettled that we
fhould meet at Lord Fortiofe's, indeed
it was to his Lordfhip that I was indebted for this, and for many other opportunities of information at Naples.

The

The houfe was emptying very faft, and I was obliged to take my leave of this fire of fong, who is the oldeft finger in Europe that continues the public exercife of his profeffion ; for he frequently fings in convents and in churches yet, though he has for fome time quitted the ftage,

In the opera to-night there were three entertaining dances, but all in the lively way; the Italians are not pleafed with any other. Indeed, as I have before obferved, all their dances are more pantomime entertainments than any thing elfe, in which the fcenes are ufually pretty, and the ftories well told. The fubject of the firft dance was *l'ifola difabitata*; of the fecond, the humours of Vauxhall Gardens in England, in which were introduced quakers, failors, women of the town, Savoyard fhew-boxes, &c. and in the third dance, at the end of the piece, the people of Thrace figured at the nuptials of Creufa and Cherinto, characters of the opera. The fix principal dancers

dancers among the men are *gli Signori Onocuto Vigano, Giuseppe Trafieri, Francesco Rafetti*; and among the women, *le Signore Colomba Beccari, Anna Torselli,* and *Caterina Ricci*; the first man has great force and neatness, and seems to equal Slingsby in his *à plomb*, or neatness of keeping time; and the Beccari's *many twinkling feet* are not inferior in agility to those of Radicate.

Monday 5. This morning I went to the Conservatorio of St. Onofrio, to see the boys take their lessons, and to hear some of the best of them play, they were all hard at work, and a noble clangor they made, not to be equalled by

> A hundred mouths, a hundred tongues,
> A hundred pair of iron lungs,
> Ten speaking trumpets, &c.

However, the ears of both master and scholar are respected when lessons in singing are given, for that work is done in a quiet room; but in the common prac-

tising

tifing rooms the noife and diffonance are beyond all conception. However, I heard in a private room two of the boys accompany each other; the one played a folo of Giardini's on the violin, and the other one of his own on the bafe; the firft was but indifferently executed, but the fecond was a pretty compofition, and very well performed. I find all over Italy that Giardini's folos, and Bach's and Abel's overtures, are in great repute, and very jufty fo, as I heard nothing equal to them of the kind, on the continent.

From hence I went to fee a great feftival at the convent of *la Donna Regina*, it was *una belliffima Funzione*, as the Italians call it, on account of two Turkifh flaves, who being converted to the Chriftian religion, were this day publicly baptifed feveral bifhops affifted at the ceremony, and the church was crowded with the beft company of Naples. The mufic was compofed by Giufeppe da Majo, a Neapolitan

litan compofer; brought up in the Confervatorio of the *Pietà*, and was excellent,
though coarfely performed.

Having the honour, to-day, of dining
at our minifter's, I was very much entertained in the afternoon by the performance of a fat friar, of the order of St.
Dominic, who came there to fing *buffo*
fongs; he accompanied himfelf on the
harpfichord in a great number of humorous fcenes from the burletta operas
of Piccini and Paefiello, which he fung
with a comic force, little inferior to that
of Cafaccia, and with a much better
voice.

Signor Nafci, who leads the band at
the comic opera in the theatre *de Fiorentini*, played on the violin in the Dominican's performance, and afterward in
fome of his own trios, which are extremely pretty, with a very uncommon
degree of grace and facility.

After this Mr Hamilton was fo obliging as to fhew me his charming picture,

painted

painted by Correggio ; the subject is a naked Venus who has taken Cupid's bow from him, which he is struggling for; while a satyr is running away with his quiver. It is a wonderful performance, and reckoned equal, for the number of figures, to the St. Jerome, at Parma.

The curiosities both of art and nature in Mr. Hamilton's possession, are numberless and inestimable. The examination of his immense collection of Etruscan vases, and other rarities of the highest antiquity, was of the utmost importance to the subject of my enquiries But by these precious remains of art I was not more enlightened, concerning the music and instruments of the ancients, than by his conversation and counsel.

When we returned to the apartments which we had quitted, in order to visit the library, we found a Neapolitan Prince and Princess, two or three ambassadors, Lord Fortrose, the French consul, a number of English gentlemen, and much other com-

company; in the evening there was more mufic, and at fupper a felect party, which did not feparate till two o'clock in the morning, when I took leave of Mr. Hamilton and his lady with infinite regret, as the countenance and affiftance with which I was honoured by them, during my refidence at Naples, were not only of the utmoft utility to me and my plan, but fuch as gratitude will never fuffer me to forget.

Tuefday 6. This day I had the honour of dining with Lord Fortrofe; the company was very numerous, and chiefly mufical. Barbella and Orgitano were invited; there was likewife the French conful, M. D'Affier. After dinner, a complete band was affembled in the gallery, and we had mufic till paft eleven o'clock. Barbella pleafed me much more to-night than he had done before; he is very certain of his tone, and has a great deal of tafte and expreffion; if he had a little more brilliancy and fullnefs of tone, and a

greater

greater variety of ftile, his playing would be unexceptionable, and perhaps fuperior to that of moft players in Europe. as it is, there feems to be a drowfinefs in his tone, and a want of animation in his manner.

Orgitano played the harpfichord, and Signor Conforte, a *mufico*, was there to fing; there was likewife a pretty good folo hautbois. The whole company had given Caffarelli over, when, behold! he arrived in great good humour, and, contrary to all expectation, was, with little entreaty, prevailed upon to fing Many notes in his voice are now thin, but there are ftill traits in his performance fufficient to convince thofe who hear him, of his having been an amazing fine finger; he accompanied himfelf, and fung without any other inftrument than the harpfichord, expreffion and grace, with great neatnefs in all he attempts, are his characteriftics. Though Caffarelli and Bar-

bella

bella are rather ancient and in ruin, yet what remains of them is but the more precious. Caffarelli propofed our fpending a whole day together, in order to difcufs mufical matters, and faid it would even be too little for all that we had to fay, but when I had acquainted him of the neceffity I was under of fetting out for Rome the next night, immediately after the opera, he offered to meet me again at Lord Fortrofe's the next morning.

After fupper, Barbella played extremely well feveral Calabrefe, Leccefe, and Neapolitan airs, and among the reft, a humourous piece compofed by himfelf, which he calls *ninna nerna*, it is a nurfery tune, or *lullaby*, excellent in its way, and was well expreffed.

Wednefday 7. I vifited by appointment Padre della Torre, to whom I had letters, he is librarian to the king, and keeper of his majefty's cabinet of rarities at the foot of Capo di Monte. I

never faw one of a more chearfully obliging character. He cannot be lefs than
70 years of age, and yet he is as lively, and even fportive, as a young man
of 20. He and his affiftant had been
hunting with great diligence in the king's
library, which formerly belonged to the
Farnefe family, and was brought hither from Parma, for materials relative
to mufic. He fhewed me, among feveral
books and MSS which I already knew,
fome curious inedited tracts which are no
where elfe to be found *.

After this, he fhewed me his microfcopes and telefcopes, which are famous
all over Italy, this father beeing faid to
have made great improvements in both,
but efpecially in microfcopes, by means of
a very fmall drop or globule of pure
chryftal glafs, the fmaller the better.

---

* There is a differtation upon found in his own
works collected and publifhed in 9 vols. 8vo.
under this title—*Elementa Phyficæ, auctore* P. D.
Johanne Maria de Terre Napoli, 1769.

He

He melts the glaſs himſelf in a veſſel of Tripoli earth, and renders it ſpherical in a clear flame. It magnifies the diameter of an object, if the globule be of the ſmalleſt claſs, 2560 times; the common microſcopes only magnify about 350 times †. After ſhewing me the whole proceſs, he was ſo obliging as to furniſh me with ſeveral of theſe glaſs globules for my own uſe.

From hence I went to the houſe of Lord Fortroſe, to meet Caffarelli; and

† The diſcovery is not new; Leeuwenhoek is ſaid to have uſed little ſpheres of glaſs in his microſcopes, Mr. Baker indeed treats them with contempt: and ſays, " Experience has taught, that they admit ſo little light, can ſhew ſuch an exceedingly " ſmall part of any object, are ſo difficult to make " uſe of, and ſtrain the eyes ſo much, that their " power of magnifying for want of due diſtinctneſs, is rather apt to produce error than diſcover truth." *Microſcope made eaſy.* But however true this might have been at the time Mr. Baker wrote, *Padre della Torre* ſeems at preſent to have got the better of every objection to theſe glaſs globules by the dexterity with which he forms and uſes them.

now I have mentioned his name for the laft time, it affords me an opportunity of acquainting my reader, that this celebrated finger has bought a dukedom for his nephew, after his own deceafe, the title is *Duca di Santi Dorato*. He is very rich, yet often fings for hire at convents and at churches He has built himfelf a magnificent houfe, and over the door is this infcription:

AMPHION THEBAS, EGO DOMVM*.

To-day I was favoured at dinner with the company of Signor Fabio, the firft violin of the opera of S. Carlo, he was fo obliging and fo humble as to bring with him his violin. It is very common in the great cities of Italy to fee performers of the firft eminence carry their own inftruments through the ftreets. This feems a trivial circumftance to mention, yet it ftrongly maiks the difference of manners and characters in two

---

* Amphion built Thebes, I only a houfe

countries

countries not very remote from each other,
In Italy, the leader of the firſt opera in
the world carries the inſtrument of his
fame and fortune about him, with as
much pride as a ſoldier does his ſword
or muſquet ; while, in England, the in-
dignities he would receive from the po-
pulace would ſoon impreſs his mind
with ſhame for himſelf and fear for his
inſtrument.

I obtained from Signor Fabio an exact
account of the number of hands employed in the great opera orcheſtra : there
are 18 firſt, and 18 ſecond violins, 5 double baſes, and but 2 violoncellos, which
I think has a bad effect, the double baſe
being played ſo coarſely throughout Italy, that it produces a ſound no more muſical than the ſtroke of a hammer. This
performer, who is a fat, good-natured
man, by being long accuſtomed to lead
ſo great a number of hands, has acquired
a ſtile of playing, which is ſomewhat
rough and inelegant, and conſequently

A a

more

more fit for an orcheftra than a chamber.
He fung, however, feveral buffo fongs
very well, and accompanied himfelf on
the violin in fo mafterly a manner, as to
produce moft of the effects of a numerous band. After dinner, he had a fecond
to accompany him in one of Giardini's
folos, and in feveral other things.

I fpent this whole evening with Barbella, who now delivered to me all the materials which he had been able to collect, relative to a hiftory of the Neapolitan confervatorios, as well as anecdotes of the
old compofers and performers of that
fchool: befides thefe, I wrote down all
the verbal information I could extract
from his memory, concerning mufical
perfons and things. During my vifit, I
heard one of his beft fcholars play a folo
of Giardini's compofition very well; he
was the moft brilliant performer on the
violin that I met with at Naples.

And now, having given the reader an
account of the mufical entertainment I

4   received

received at Naples, I hope I shall be indulged with the liberty of making a few reflexions before I quit this city; which has so long been regarded as the centre of harmony, and the fountain from whence genius, taste, and learning, have flowed to every other part of Europe; that even those who have an opportunity of judging for themselves, take upon trust the truth of the fact, and give the Neapolitans credit for more than they deserve at present, however they may have been entitled to this celebrity in times past.

M. de la Lande's account of music at Naples, is so far from exact, that it would incline his reader to suppose one of two things, either that he did not attend to it, or that he had not a very distinguishing ear.

" Music, says this author, is in a par-
" ticular manner the triumph of the
" Neapolitans, it seems as if the tym-
" panum in this country was more bra-

ced,

" ced, more harmonical, and more fono-
" rous, than in the reft of Europe; the
" whole nation is vocal, every gefture
" and inflexion of voice of the inhabi-
" tants, and even their profody of fyl-
" lables in converfation, breathe har-
" mony and mufic. Hence Naples is
" the principal fource of Italian mufic,
" of great compofers, and of excellent
" operas *."

I am ready to grant that the Neapolitans have a natural difpofition to mufic; but can by no means allow that they
have voices more flexible, and a language
more harmonious than the inhabitants
of the other parts of Italy, as the direct
contrary feems true. The finging in the

---

* *Voyage du'n Françoi*, Tom 6 The inaccu-
racy with which M de la L fpeaks about mufic
and muficians, runs through his work. He
places Corelli and Galuppi among the Neapolitan
Compofers, whereas it is well known that Corelli was of the Roman fchool, and he himfelf
fays in another place (Tom. 5) that Galuppi was
of the Venetian

ftreets

ſtreets is far leſs pleaſing, though more original than elſewhere ; and the Neapolitan language is generally ſaid to be the moſt barbarous jargon among all the different dialects of Italy *.

But though the riſing generation of Neapolitan muſicians cannot be ſaid to poſſeſs either taſte, delicacy, or expreſſion, yet their compoſitions, it muſt be allowed, are excellent with reſpect to counter-point and invention ; and in their manner of executing them, there is an energy and fire, not to be met with perhaps in the whole univerſe . it is ſo ardent as to border upon fury , and from this impetuoſity of genius, it is common for a Neapolitan compoſer, in a movement which begins in a mild and ſober manner, to ſet the orcheſtra in

* A ſufficient proof of the Neapolitan language being only a *patois* or provincial dialect, is, that it remains merely oral, the natives themſelves, who are well educated, never daring to write in it.

flames

flames before it is finished. Dr Johnson says, that Shakespeare, in tragedy, is always struggling after some occasion to be comic, and the Neapolitans, like high bred horses, are impatient of the rein, and eagerly accelerate their motion to the utmost of their speed. The pathetic and the graceful are seldom attempted in the conservatorios ; and those refined and studied graces, which not only change, but improve passages, and which so few are able to find, are less sought after by the generality of performers at Naples, than in any other part of Italy.

R O M E.

Sunday, Nov. 11. Having a little recovered the fatigue of my journey from Naples, I renewed my operations at Rome.

This morning I went to the convent of St. Ursula, to see a nun take the veil.

The

The company was very numerous, and compofed chiefly of the firft people of Rome, who were all in full drefs I was placed clofe to the altar, where I could fee the whole ceremony, and hear every word that was uttered. The fervice was begun by faying mafs, then cardinal de Roffi entered in great ftate , while the organ was playing, and the mafs was finging : the mufic both vocal and inftrumental, was performed by the nuns and ladies of the convent, who were placed in the organ gallery. The compofition was pretty, but ill executed ; the organ was a bad one, and too powerful for the band : moft of the beft hands, as I was informed, were occupied in the convent with the internal ceremony, the external was all performed in the chapel.

When the cardinal was robed, the noviciate was led into the chapel by a lady of the firft rank in Rome, and brought to the altar in exceeding high drefs. Her hair was of a beautiful light brown, and

curled

curled *en tête de mouton* all over her head.
Her gown was of the richeft embroidered;
and, I believe, emboffed blue and filver, I
ever faw. She had on a large ftage hoop;
and a great quantity of diamonds, the
train of her robe dragged full two yards
on the ground ; fhe feemed rather a pretty fort of young perfon than a beauty.
When fhe firft appeared, fhe looked very
pale, and more dead than alive ; fhe
made a moft profound reverence to the
cardinal, who was feated on the fteps of
the altar in his mitre and all his rich
veftments, ready to receive her. She threw
herfelf upon her knees at the foot of the
altar, and remained in that pofture fome
time, while other parts of the ceremony
were adjufting ; then fhe walked up to
the cardinal, who faid, *Figlia mia, che do-
mandate ?* My child, what is your requeft? She faid, that fhe begged to be
admitted into that convent as a fifter of
the order of St Urfula. Have you well,
faid the cardinal, confidered of what you
ask,

áfk ? She anfwered, chearfully, that fhe had; and was well informed of all fhe was about to do Then fhe kneeled down again, and kiffed the cardinal's hands, and received from him a little crucifix, which fhe alfo kiffed; after which fhe retired again to the foot of the altar, where fhe threw herfelf on her knees, while the cardinal faid mafs, which was fung at the fame time in the organ loft. After this, there was a fermon in the Italian language, and that being over, the cardinal led the nun-elect into the convent, where fhe was divefted of all her gorgeous attire and worldly vanities, and had her hair cut off. She then came to the gate in her religious drefs, to receive the white veil, with which fhe was invefted by the lady ab-befs, the cardinal and the other affiftants ftanding by.

After this there was more pretty mufic badly performed. The organ, by execut-ing all the fymphonies and accompaniments,

ménts, overpowered the violins, and had a
bad effect, though neatly played.

When her veil was on, the new sister
came to the convent door, to receive the
congratulations of her friends and of the
company; but first, with a lighted taper
in her hand, she went round the convent
to salute all the nuns, who had likewise
tapers in their hands. When she was at
the door, with the veil and crown on, but
her face uncovered, I, among the rest,
went close to her, and found she was
much prettier than I had before imagined.
She had a sweet mouth, and the finest
teeth in the world, with lively sparkling
eyes, and a genteel shaped visage, she
would, any where else, have been stiled
a very pretty woman, but here, so cir-
cumstanced, a beauty. At the altar she
changed countenance several times, first
pale, then red, and seemed to pant, and
to be in danger of either bursting into
tears, or fainting; but she recovered before the ceremony was ended, and at the

convent

convent door affumed an air of great chearfulnefs, talked to feveral of her friends and acquaintance, and feemed to give up the world very heroically.——And thus ended this human facrifice!

In the afternoon I went to the Chiefa Nuova, to hear an oratorio in that church, where the facred drama took its rife. There are two galleries; in one there is an organ, and in the other a harpfichord; in the former the fervice was begun by the matins in four parts, *alla Palestrina*, then the *Salve Regina* was fung *a voce fola*, after which there were prayers, and then a little boy, not above fix years old, mounted the pulpit, and delivered a difcourfe, by way of fermon, which he had got by heart, and which was rendered truly ridiculous by the vehicle through which it paffed. The oratorio of Abigail, fet to mufic by Signor Cafali, was then performed. This drama confifted of four characters, and was divided into two parts. The two firft

move-

movements of the overture pleafed me very much, the laft not at all. It was, as ufual, a minuet degenerated into a jigg of the moft common caft. This rapidity in the minuets of all modern overtures renders them ungraceful at an opera, but in a church they are indecent. The reft of the mufic was pretty common place, for though it could boaft of no new melody or modulation, it had nothing vulgar in it.

Signor Criftofero fung the principal part very well, in Guarducci's fmooth and polifhed manner. He made two or three excellent clofes, though they were rather too long; this fault is general throughout Rome and Naples, where fuch a long-winded licentioufnefs prevails in the cadences of every finger, as is always tirefome, and often difgufting; even thofe of great performers need compreffion, and thofe made by performers of an inferior clafs not only want curtailing, but correction. A few felect notes

with

with a great deal of meaning and expreffion given to them, is the only expedient that can render a cadence defirable,
as it fhould confift of fomething *fuperior*
to what has been heard in the air, or it
becomes impertinent. This abufe in
making clofes is not of very ancient ftanding, for in a ferious opera of old Scarlatti,
compofed in 1717, there is not a fingle
place for a cadence *ad libitum* to be
found.

Between the two parts of this oratorio,
there was a fermon by a Jefuit, delivered
from the fame pulpit from whence the
child had defcended. I waited to hear
the laft chorus, which, though it was
fung by book, was as light and as un-
meaning as an opera chorus, which muft
be got by heart. With refpect to a true
oratorio chorus accompanied with inftruments in the manner of Handel's, I heard
but few all the time I was in Italy.
When this performance was over, I went,

as usual, to the Duke of Dorset's concert.

Monday 12 I visited the Pope's, or Sistine chapel, and being a day in which there was no service, I had permission to go into every part of it, which I was curious to do on many accounts. First, as it was the place in which the famous *Miserere* of Allegri is performed, secondly, as it was here that church-music first had its rise, and was brought to its highest perfection; and thirdly, where, at the altar piece, is so wonderfully painted the last judgment: it is the greatest work of Michael Angelo, and perhaps of man. Nothing can be conceived more astonishing and dreadful than the ideas and figures which his dark imagination has produced: neither the *Inferno* of Dante, nor the hell of Milton, can furnish any thing more terrible. But this amazing work is greatly discoloured, and the ceiling, by the same painter, is in many

places

places broken down, two or three feet in breadth. The fides are painted by Pietro Perugino, and are the beft works I have feen of this famous mafter of the divine Raphael.

I went up into the orcheftra with refpect-ful curiofity, to fee the place facred to the works of Paleftrina. It feems hardly large enough to contain thirty performers, the ordinary number of fingers in the Pope's fervice; and yet, on great feftivals, fuper-numeraries are added to thefe. There was nothing in the orcheftra now but a large wooden defk, for the fcore book of the maeftro di Capella, and marble feats at the back and fides: it is placed on the right hand in approaching the altar, facing the Pope's throne, which is near the altar on the other fide. There are feats or ftalls for the cardinals at the fides of the chapel and a fmall place for ambaffadors to ftand in, juft within the rails oppofite to the altar; but no other ftrangers are ever admitted; nor are any perfons, except the performers,

fuffered

suffered to enter the orcheftra during the fervice. The grate, or baluftrade, which is in diamond fquares, gilt, feems to take off one third of the whole room, which is very lofty and magnificent, but now very dufty and much out of repair; the floor is in beautiful Mofaic of marble.

From hence I went to the Pauline chapel, which is ufed only once a year, at which time it is illuminated with many thoufand lamps.

In the afternoon I had the pleafure of feeing my very good friend Signor Santa-relli, who had not only bufied himfelf in feeking curious things for me during my abfence at Naples, but had employed feveral perfons in tranfcribing them; the Abate Elie had done the fame at the Vatican; and the Cavalier Piranefi, my Englifh friends, and feveral eminent an-tiquaries and artifts had been active in fearching ancient inftruments, among the *baffi rilievi* and beft fculptures of antiqui-ty, and copying them ready for me at my

return

return to Rome. Signor Santarelli was
fo obliging as to accompany me to the
Cavalier Battoni's, where his fcholar, the
Signorina Battoni, fung with noble fimplicity, and a truly pathetic expreffion,
feveral fongs of Haffe, Galuppi, Traetta,
and Piccini.

From hence I went to a great concert, at the houfe of M. Schovelhoffe,
the Mofcovite general; and there I almoft fancied myfelf in London; for,
except three or four, the whole company,
confifting of near thirty noblemen, gentlemen, and ladies, was Englifh. The
little Mignatrici, Bichelli, was there to
fing, and another girl, the former fung
very well, and the other *will* fing, fome
time hence: there was nothing extraordinary in the inftruments.

Tuefday 13. I had but juft time to
ftep into the beautiful little church of
St. Andrea della Noviciata, built by
Bernini, at which there was mufic compofed by Orificcchio, and led by Nicolai;

B b   but,

but, though my ftay was very fhort, I heard a *finfonia* or overture, and a chorus a *due cori*, which were excellent*.

Friday 16. In a vifit I made Signor San-tarelli this morning, I found with him three or four of his brethren of the pope's chapel; among the reft, Signor Pafquale Pifari, who had with him the original fcore of a mafs in 16 real parts, which was full of canons, fugues, and imita-tions: I never faw a more learned or in-genious compofition of the kind. Pa-leftrina never wrote in more than eight real parts, and few have fucceeded in fo many as thofe; but to double the number is infinitely more than doubling the dif-ficulties. After three parts, the addition of another becomes more and more diffi-cult; all that can be done on thefe oc-cafions, is to adhere to a fimple melody

---

* Signor Orificchio ranks fo high among the prefent Roman compofers for the church, that upon any feftival wherever he is Maeftro di Capella, and has compofed a mafs, there is fure to be a very great crowd

and

and modulation, and to keep the parts as
much as poffible in contrary, or at leaft,
diffimilar motion. In the compofition
of Signor Pifari, every fpecies of contrivance is fuccefsfully ufed. Sometimes the parts anfwer or imitate each
other, by two and two; fometimes the
fubjects are inverted in fome of the parts,
while their original order is preferved in
others. A century or two ago, the author of fuch a compofition would have
had a ftatue erected to his honour; but
now, it would be equally difficult to find
16 people who would hear it with patience, as that number of good fingers, in
any one place, to perform it. Befides
vocal parts in this mafs, there is a part
for the organ, often on a regular fubject, different from the reft: the ground-
work, upon which all is built, is *canto
fermo*; and, in fome of the movements, this canto fermo is made a fubject of imitation, and runs through all
the parts. Upon the whole, it muft be

allowed, that this work, which confifts of many different movements, and is of a very confiderable length, though it may be thought by fome to require more patience than genius to accomplifh, feems fufficient to have employed a long life in compofing, and to entitle the author to great praife and admiration.

During this vifit, which was my laft to Signor Santarelli, he and his brethren of the pope's chapel, were fo obliging as to execute feveral beautiful compofitions of Paleftrina, Benevoli, and Allegri, in order to give me a true idea of the delicate and expreffive manner in which they are fung in the chapel of his holinefs.

In the afternoon I went to Signor Crifpi's *accademia*; I arrived late, while fome new *Quartettos* of his compofition were performing; but he was fo obliging as to defire the band to begin again, and to go through with the whole fix. I think thefe pieces have great merit, and are fuperior to any of his other productions.

Sunday

Sunday 18. I went this morning with Mr. Wyfeman to the church of S. John Lateran *; it is the moft antient church in Chriftendom. I here heard high mafs performed in the Colonna chapel, by two choirs, and faw it played by Signor Colifta, the celebrated organift of that church, on a little moveable organ. The mufic was by Signor Cafali, Maeftro di Capella, who was there to beat time. I was introduced both to him and to Signor Colifta, after the fervice; and the latter upon being entreated to let me hear the great organ, very obligingly confented,

---

* Mr. Wyfeman is a worthy Englifh muficmafter, who is well known and efteemed by all the Englifh at Rome, where he has fo long been an inhabitant, that he has almoft forgot his native tongue. He now lives in the *Palazzo Rafaele*, without the gates of Rome; where, during the firft winter months, he has a concert every week till the operas begin. It was here that the great Raphael lived, where there are ftill fome of his paintings in frefco, and where the late Duke of York, the Prince of Brunfwick, and feveral other great perfonages, gave concerts to the firft people of Rome.

B b 3 upon

upon condition that *Monfignore al Pre-fetto* of the church was applied to; which is a neceffary ceremony in confe-quence of fome injury formerly done. to the inftrument, by the malice or ig-norance of a 'ftranger who had played' upon it. This application was readily undertaken, and the permiffion obtained, by Signor Cafali.

I was conducted into the great organ-loft by Signor Colifta, who did me the favour to open the cafe, and to fhew me all the internal conftruction of this famous inftrument It is a thirty-two feet organ, and the largeft in Rome. It was firft built in 1549, and has under-gone two repairs fince, the one in 1600, by Luca Blafi Perugino, and a fecond, a few years fince, under the direction of the prefent organift. It has thirty-fix ftops, two fets of keys, long eighths, an octave below double F. and goes up to E. in altiffimo It has likewife pedals, in the ufe of which Signor Colifta is very dex-trous.

trous. His manner of playing this inftrument feems to be the true organ ftile, though his tafte is rather ancient; indeed the organ ftile feems to be better preferved throughout Italy than it is with us; as the harpfichord is not fufficiently cultivated to encroach upon that inftrument. Signor Colifta played feveral fugues, in which the fubjects were frequently introduced on the pedals, in a very mafterly manner. But it feems as if every virtue in mufic was to border upon fome vice; for this ftile of playing precludes all grace, tafte, and melody; while the light, airy harpfichord kind of playing, deftroys the *foftenuto* and richnefs of harmony and contrivance of which this divine inftrument is fo peculiarly capable.

It is very extraordinary that the *fwell*, which has been introduced into the Englifh organ more than fifty years, and which is fo capable of expreffion and of pleafing effects, that it may well be faid

to

to be the greateſt and moſt important improvement that ever was made on any keyed inſtrument, ſhould be ſtill utterly unknown in Italy*. The *touch* too of the organ, which our builders have ſo much improved, ſtill remains in its heavy, noiſy ſtate; and now I am on this ſubject, I muſt obſerve, that moſt of the organs I have met with on the Continent, ſeem to be inferior to ours built by father Smith, Byfield, or Snetzler, in every thing but ſize. As the churches there are often immenſe, ſo are the organs; the tone is indeed ſomewhat ſoftened and refined by ſpace and diſtance; but when heard near, it is intolerably coarſe and noiſy; and though the number of ſtops in theſe

---

* It is the fame with the *Beat* upon the uniſon, octave, or any conſonant found to a note on the violin, which ſo well ſupplies the place of the old cloſe-ſhake. for this beautiful effect, if not wholly unknown, is at leaſt neglected by all the violin performers I heard on the continent, though ſo commonly and ſucceſsfully practiſed in England by thoſe of the Giardini ſchool.

large

large inftruments is very great, they afford but little variety, being, for the moft
part, duplicates in unifons and octaves to
each-other, fuch as the great and fmall
12ths,-flutes, and 15ths: hence in our-or-
gans not only the touch and tone, but the
imitative ftops are greatly fuperior to thofe
of any other organs I have met with.

Immediately after dinner I went to St.
Peter's, where there was a great *Funzione*
for the feaft of it's foundation. The vefpers were faid by Cardinal York, affifted
by feveral bifhops: there were Mazzanti
and Criftofero to fing, befides feveral other
fupernumeraries, and the whole choir.
The fat Giovannini, famous for playing
the violoncello, as well as for being one
of the *maeftri di capella* of St Peter's, beat
time. The folo parts were finely fung
by the two fingers juft mentioned, and the
choruffes by two choirs, and two organs,
were admirably performed. Part of the
mufic was by Paleftrina, part by Benevoli,
and the reft modern, but in a grave and
majeftic

majeftic ftile. I never heard church mufic, except that of the Pope's chapel, fo
well performed. There were no other
inftruments than the two organs, four
violoncellos, and two double bafes. Some
fugues and imitations in dialogue between
the two choirs were performed, which
had a very fine effect. The fervice was
in the large canonical, or winter chapel
on the left, in which is the largeft organ
of St Peter's church *.

Cardinal York faid mafs likewife in the
morning, when there was a great congregation.

At night I went to the oratorio of
Jonathan, at the Chiefa Nuova; but
not being either well fet or well fung, I
quitted that performance at the end of the
firft part, in order to hear another at the
church of St Gerolamo della Carità,

* There are no other organs, nor indeed choirs
at St Peter's than thofe in the fide chapels, fo that
the diftance between the weft door and the great
altar, is wholly a free and unbroken fpace.

which

which had only three characters in it,
this oratorio was called the Judgment of
Solomon : the tenor finger in it was admirable; he had great taste, and a very
uncommon facility of execution: a eu-
nuch likewise, who performed the part
of one of the mothers, had a sweet toned
voice, and sung in a very pleasing manner. The subject seems to be extremely
well adapted for musical expression : the
sternness of the judge; the indifference of
the false mother ; and the tenderness of
the true, are severally susceptible of different musical colouring and expression.
The music, which had merit, was by a
young composer who had begged employment in order to have an opportunity
of displaying his talents : his name is
Giuseppe Maria Magherini.

Tuesday 20. I went this morning to
visit the famous Podini gallery, in the Ve-
rufpi palace. All the accounts of Rome
are full of the praises of this music gallery, or, as it is called, gallery of instruments,

ments; but nothing shews the neceffity of feeing for one's felf, more than thefe accounts. The inftruments in queftion cannot have been fit for ufe thefe many years; but, when a thing has once got into a book as curious, it is copied into others without examination, and without end. There is a very fine harpfichord, to look at, but not a key that will fpeak: it formerly had a communication with an organ in the fame room, and with two fpinets and a virginal; under the frame is a violin, tenor, and bafe, which, by a movement of the foot, ufed to be played upon by the harpfichord keys. The organ appears in the front of the room, but not on the fide, where there feems to be pipes and machines enclofed; but there was no one to open or explain it, the old *Ciceroni* being juft dead.

Wednefday 21. This morning I went to the Kirkeana mufeum, founded about the middle of the laft century by Father Kircher, author of the *Mufurgia*, and of

feveral

several other curious and learned work
Mr. Morrison, who had obtained permission for me to see it, was so obliging as
to accompany me thither. The museo
was shewn us by a young Irish jesuit, Father Plunket, I think, who is likewise a
young antiquary; but Mr. Morrison,
who is undoubtedly one of the first and
most sagacious antiquaries in Rome, set
him right in many particulars. Ancient
paintings, urns, vases, jewels, intaglios,
cameos, and other antiquities, are here
in such abundance, that I could have fancied myself at Portici; but the curiosities
I chiefly went to see, were Father Kircher's musical instruments and machines,
described in his *Musurgia*: they are now almost all out of order, but their construction
is really curious, and manifests the ingenuity as well as zeal of this learned father
in his musical enquiries and experiments.

In visiting Rome a second time, I took
a view of the theatres, of which there are

7   seven

feven or eight: the principal are the *Argentina*, the *Aliberti*, the *Pordinone*, and the *Capranica*: the two firſt are very large, and appropriated to ſerious operas. The *Pordenone* theatre is uſed as a play-houſe for tragedies and comedies; and the *Capranica* for burlettas, or comic operas.

There are no public ſpectacles allowed in Rome, except during carnival time, which laſts from the ſeventh of January to Aſh-Wedneſday; nor are any women ever ſuffered to appear upon the ſtage, the female characters being repreſented by eunuchs, and frequently ſo well, from their delicacy of voice and figure, as to deceive perſons unacquainted with this prohibition.

- Rome is the poſt of honour for compoſers, the Romans being the moſt faſtidi-ous judges of muſic in *Italy*. There is like-wiſe in this city more cabal than elſewhere, and party runs higher. It is generally ſuppoſed, that a compoſer or performer who

who is fuccefsful at Rome, has nothing
to fear from the feverity of critics in
other places. At the opening of an opera,
the clamour or acclamation of the company frequently continues for a confiderable time before they will hear a note.
A favourite author is received with fhouts
of *Bravo! Signor Maeftro. Viva! Signor
Maeftro.* And when a compofer is condemned by the audience, it is with difcrimination in favour of the finger, by
crying out, after they have done hiffing,
Bravo! pure, il Guarducci *! and on the
contrary, if the performer difpleafes in
executing the mufic of a favourite compofer, after they have expreffed their
difapprobation of him, by hiffing, they
cry out *Viva! pure, il Signor Maeftro.*

It was with much regret that I quitted
this venerable city, which is no lefs delightful to ftrangers for the innumerable
rarities it offers to their view, than for

---

* Bravo! however, Guarducci.

the eafy and focial manner in which they live with the natives, as well as with each other.

I have now given an account of the ftate of mufic in the principal cities of Italy; there are, however, many places which I either was unable to vifit, or in which my ftay was too fhort to obtain much information; however, the following particulars feem worthy of being mentioned : at Loretto there is a confiderable mufic fchool : at Siena there are curious miffals: at Pifa, mufic is in a flourifhing ftate, as I was informed, upon the fpot, by Signor Lidarti, who lives there; Signor Gualberto Brunetti is Maeftro di Capella at the cathedral; and Gherardefchi, Renzini, Lidarti, and Corrucci, are eminent compofers in that city.

At Perugia Signor Zanetti has long refided; but he loft his place of Maeftro di Capella to the great church there, lately, by having appeared on the Aliberti ftage at Rome, as a finger in an ope-

ra

ra of his own compofition, and that, merely to fupply the place of the principal tenor, who had run away, and to prevent the piece from being ftopt: he is fince married to a pretty woman, who fings well, and is likely to indemnify him for the lofs of his place.

At Parma, Signor Poncini is compofer to the great church, as is Signor Colla to the prince; and Signor Ferrara, brother to the famous violin player, who is a remarkable fine performer on the violoncello; together with the celebrated finger Baftardini, and Signora Roger, a great harpfichord player, who was miftrefs to the princefs of Afturias, are all in penfion at the court of Parma. The theatre there is the largeft in Europe; it is capable of containing four thoufand people, and has water under the ftage fufficient to form a great river, or for the reprefentation of a fea-fight; but this theatre has not been ufed fince the death of the laft duke.

In

In arriving at Genoa, I found no other public mufical performance than an *intermezzo*, in which Piatti, a young finger who had juft returned from England, was principal.

From the number of mufical eftablifhments and performances mentioned in this journal, the Italians may, perhaps, be accufed of cultivating mufic to excefs; but whoever continues a fhort time in any of their principal cities, muft perceive that other arts and fciences are not neglected: and even in travelling through the country, if the Ecclefiaftical State be excepted, the natural fertility of the foil does not appear to be the only fource of abundance in the neceffaries of life; for I can venture to affirm, that, throughout Lombardy and Tufcany, agriculture is carried on with fuch art and activity, that I never remember to have feen lands better laid out, or lefs frequently fuffered to lie idle: the poor, indeed, are oppref-

4   fed

-fed and rendered worthlefs by the rigour pf government; but were they lefs fo under their Gothic tyrants, when arts and fciences were not only neglected but extirpated from among them? Perhaps the cultivation of the peaceful arts may contribute as much to the happinefs of the prefent inhabitants of Italy, and, indeed, of the reft of the world, as the conquering kingdoms did to that of their martial anceftors; who, when they were not bufied in cutting the throats of each other, employed all their time and talents in plundering and enflaving mankind.

But mufic is now thought neceffary in every country in Europe; and if it *muft* be had, why fhould it not be excellent? The fuperior refinement of the Italian mufic cannot be fairly attributed to the great number of *artificial* voices with which Italy, to its difhonour, abounds; for vocal mufic feems at prefent in its higheft ftate of perfection in the confervatorios of Venice, where only the *natural* voices

of

of females can be heard; fo that the greateft crime of which the Italians feem guilty is the having dared to apply to their fofter language, a fpecies of mufic more delicate and refined, than the reft of Europe can boaft.

It is now time to clofe my account of the prefent ftate of mufic in Italy, in doing which I cannot diffemble my fears that the reader will think it prolix; as, upon revifing my journal, I am forry to find that the further I advanced into that country, the more loofe is the texture of my narrative; for in proportion as I had more to hear and to fee, I had lefs time to fpare for reflection and for writing: indeed, the mere matters of fact concerning mufical exhibitions, will, I doubt, afford but fmall entertainment to the reader; for they are fo much the fame, that an account of one is, in many particulars, an account of all; fo that a circumftantial narrative of things, perhaps not very interefting in themfelves, might be

tirefome

tirefome even in fpight of variety: all I
have to urge in my defence, is, that the re-
lation is faithful, and that, if the places,
through which I paffed had afforded
more entertaining incidents, they would
have been given to the public.

After a very fatiguing and dangerous
journey over the tremendous mountains of
Genoa, and through Provence and Languedoc, during inceffant rains which had
rendered the roads intolerable, I arrived
at Lyons in my way home, Dec. 3d,
where, in vifiting the theatre, I was more
difgufted than ever, at hearing French
mufic, after the exquifite performances to
which I had been accuftomed in Italy.
Eugenie, a pretty comedy, preceded Sil-
vain, an opera by M. Gretry: there were
many pretty paffages in the mufic, but
fo ill fung, with fo falfe an expreffion, fuch
fcreaming, forcing, and trilling, as quite
made me fick.

I tried to obferve, on the road, by what
degrees the French arrive at this extreme

de-

depravity in their mufical expreffion, and
I find, that in defcending the Alps, it does
not come on all at once. In Provence
and Languedoc, the tunes of the country
people are rather pretty; I prevailed on
them to fing me fome wherever I ftopt,
which they did in a natural and fimple
manner. The airs are lefs wild than the
Scots, as lefs ancient, but I rather think
the melodies of Provence and Languedoc
are older than any now fubfifting that
were formed upon the fyftem of Guido.

From Lyons I travelled night and day
to Paris, and arrived there on Saturday,
Dec. 8th; but I fhall detain my reader
no longer with obfervations upon French
mufic, of which the expreffion is notori-
oufly hateful to all the people in Europe
but themfelves. however, in the midft
of this feeming feverity of decifion, it is
but juft to own, that the French have as
long known the mechanical laws of counter-point as any nation in Europe; and, that
at prefent, by means of M. Rameau's fyftem

and

and rules for a fundamental bafe, they are very good judges of harmony. It muft likewife be allowed, that they have long been in poffeffion of fimple and agreeable Provençale and Languedocian melodies, to which they continue to adapt the prettieft words, for focial purpofes, of any people on the globe, and that they have now the merit of imitating very fuccefsfully the mufic of the Italian burlettas, in their comic operas, and of greatly furpaffing the Italians, and, perhaps, every other nation, in the poetical compofition of thofe dramas.

During my laft refidence at Paris, I had the honour of conferring with many men of letters of the firft clafs, whofe opennefs and politenefs to me were fuch as merit my moft grateful and public acknowledgments; and I cannot refift the defire of mentioning two, among thefe, of a very diftinguifhed order, M. Diderot, and M. Rouffeau.

With M. Diderot, I had the happinefs of converfing feveral times; and I was

C c 4   pleafed

pleafed to find, that among all the fciences which his extenfive genius and
learning have inveftigated, there is no one
that he interefts himfelf more about,
than mufic. Mademoifelle Diderot, his
daughter, is one of the fineft harpfi-
chord-players in Paris, and, for a lady,
poffeffed of an uncommon portion of
knowledge in modulation; but though I
had the pleafure of hearing her for feveral hours, not a fingle French compofition was played by her the whole time,
all was Italian and German; hence
it will not be difficult to form a judgment of M. Diderot's tafte in mufic.
He entered fo zealoufly into my views
concerning the hiftory of his favourite
art, that he prefented me with a number
of his own MSS. fufficient for a volume
in folio on the fubject. Thefe, from fuch
a writer, I regard as invaluable; " Here,
" take them, fays he, I know not what
" they contain, if any materials for your
" purpofe, ufe them in the courfe of
" your

" your work, as your own property; if
" not, throw them into the fire." But
notwithstanding such a legal transfer, I
shall look upon myself as accountable for
these papers, not only to M. Diderot, but
to the public.

I regarded the meeting with M. Rouffeau at Paris, as a fingularly fortunate
completion of my perfonal intercourfe
with the learned and ingenious on the
continent: I was fo happy as to converfe
for a confiderable time with him upon
mufic, a fubject which has received fuch
embellifhments from his pen, that the
dryeft parts of it are rendered interefting
by his manner of treating them, both in
the Encyclopedie, and in his Mufical
Dictionary. He read over my plan very
attentively, and gave me his opinion of
it, article by article; after which he
made enquiries concerning feveral Italian
compofers of his acquaintance, and feemed to intereft himfelf very much about
the prefent ftate of mufic in Italy, as
well

well as the acquisitions I had made there towards my future work.

* * * *

The reader of this journal will now be enabled not only to form an idea of the prefent ftate of mufic in the countries through which I have paffed, but likewife of the opportunities with which I have been favoured of confulting the libraries and the learned, on whatever is moft difputable and curious in my projeded hiftory. I have mentioned fome of the materials which I acquired, and to thefe may be added a great number, which I colleded during many years in England, and near 400 volumes of fcarce books on the fubjed of mufic, which I procured abroad. I have alfo fettled a correfpondence in every great city that I vifited on the continent, by means of which I hope to be furnifhed from time to time with the neweft intelligence concerning modern mufic, as well as with further

par-

particulars, relative to the ancient; and
as I am certain that no place abounds.
more with men of found learning, or
with collectors of curious compofitions
and valuable materials neceffary to my
intended work, than my own country;
I humbly hope that I fhall alfo be
honoured with their counfel and commu-
nications.

But with all thefe requifites, refpect
for the public, for the art about which I,
write, and even for myfelf, will prevent.
precipitate publication : a hiftory of the
kind I propofe, muft inevitably be a,
work of time; for after confulting the
moft fcarce and valuable books and MSS.
and conferring with the moft eminent
artifts and theorifts; to felect, digeft, and
confolidate materials fo various and dif-
fufed, will not only require leifure and
labour, but fuch a patient perfeverance, as
little lefs than the zeal of enthufiafm can
infpire. It is not the hiftory of an art
in its infant ftate, whofe parents are ftill
living,

living, that I have ventured to under-
take ; but one coeval with the world ;
one whofe high antiquity renders its
origin as doubtful, as the formation of
language, or the firft articulations of the
human voice.

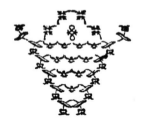

I N D E X.

Bocchirini,

INDEX.

Conti,

D d

Ligniville,

INDEX.

I   *Mufic*

Painting,

INDEX.

INDEX.

Vallotti,

INDEX.

F I N I S.

ADVERTISEMENT.

A General Plan of the author's intended
History of Music, with Proposals
for Printing it by Subscription, will be submitted to the public as soon as the work is
sufficiently advanced to enable him to fix a
time with any degree of certainty for its
appearance.